D0871110

Mission of the Church

Mission of the Church

Essays on Practical Theology for
21st Century Ministry

Edited by
Jerome Boone, Jerald Daffe,
William Effler, and Henry Smith

WIPF & STOCK · Eugene, Oregon

MISSION OF THE CHURCH
Essays on Practical Theology for 21st Century Ministry

Wipf & Stock
An Imprint of Wipf and Stock Publishers
199 W. 8th Ave., Suite 3
Eugene, OR 97401

www.wipfandstock.com

PAPERBACK ISBN: 978-1-5326-4188-6
HARDCOVER ISBN: 978-1-5326-4189-3
EBOOK ISBN: 978-1-5326-4190-9

Manufactured in the U.S.A.

Contents

Acknowledgments

THIS PROJECT COULD NOT have been successfully created without the contributions made by the Christian Ministries faculty of the School of Religion at Lee University in Cleveland, Tennessee. I sincerely appreciate each of my colleagues for their creative efforts in this volume, namely, Bob Bayles, Jerome Boone, Terry Cross, Rolando Cuellar, Jerald Daffe, Thomas Doolittle, Jimmy Harper, John Lombard, Lisa Long, Edley Moodley, Henry Smith, and Mark Walker.

Special thanks to Jerome Boone, Jerald Daffe, and Henry Smith, who have served as the editorial committee and contributed extensively to the development of the manuscript. Thank you to Courtney Foster and Melissa Melching for their tireless efforts in the final formatting.

Bill Effler, DMin
General Editor
Fall 2017

Introduction

WHERE DOES ONE BEGIN when asking the question, "What is the mission of the church?" For me, it begins with Jesus, the Author and, one day, the Finisher of our faith.[1] Jesus began his mission with an end goal clearly in sight. The goal was that his mission would one day become the mission of the modern church.[2] His inaugural message was based on a Scripture found in the scrolls of the prophet Isaiah.[3] Because Jesus began his ministry founded on Scripture, we must know that the use and application of Scripture is to be held in high regard in the mission of the church. Below is an introductory overview of this prophecy as one way of beginning to answer the question, "What is the mission of the church?"[4]

Jesus' mission (as described in Isaiah 61) begins with the bold declaration, "The Spirit of the Lord is upon me."[5] The mission of any church, and really the life of any individual, must begin with this very same conviction. Every expression of a church's mission and ministry builds on this guiding principle. This non-negotiable imperative teaches that it is the Spirit who orchestrates and calls forth both corporate ministry and individual renewal. The sovereign activity of God, a "blowing where it wills,"[6] is for the purpose of renewing all people regardless of gender, ethnicity, cultural context or station in life.[7] When the Holy Spirit of God comes upon

---

1. Heb 12:2.

2. The concept of "beginning with the end in mind" was first coined by Stephen Covey in his book, *Seven Habits of Highly Successful People.*

3. Luke 4:18–19.

4. Words or phrases that are italicized throughout my introduction represent different aspects or expressions of "the Mission of the Church."

5. Isa 61:1a.

6. John 3:8.

7. Gal 3:28.

a person, that person will be convicted of sin,[8] sanctified in the core of the being,[9] and baptized into the family of God.[10] Furthermore, this individual will be guided in everyday decision-making,[11] receive spiritual gifts for the purpose of advancing the mission of Jesus,[12] and will see that God will produce in their life "fruit that will last."[13]

Following the unshakable assurance that God's Spirit is "upon" an individual (and churches), Isaiah continues by prophesying that the Lord's Spirit has been given, in part, to proclaim good news to the broken, the captive, and the prisoner.[14] One can correlate Isaiah's Old Testament prophecy of proclaiming good news to the New Testament ministry of proclamation and evangelism as documented in the book of Acts and throughout the writings of the Apostle Paul. It must be noted that Jesus told his disciples to wait in Jerusalem for the coming of the Holy Spirit before ever saying a word: "you will receive power when the Holy Spirit comes on you; and you will be my witnesses in Jerusalem, and in all Judea and Samaria, and to the ends of the earth."[15] The gift of the Spirit, says Jesus, is for the expressed purpose of empowering God's people so they can be used as witnesses throughout the world. I would add here that churches seeking to have a "voice" in their communities should be cognizant that the Apostle Paul told the Corinthian church that speaking words without love is just noise.[16]

Isaiah continues by declaring that comfort is to be given to the afflicted.[17] The prophet announces that there will be "joy where there was once despair"[18] and that "disgrace will be replaced with a double portion of inheritance."[19] One may interpret this prophetic promise to be a reference to the ministry of pastoral care, spiritual formation, or the ministry of

8. John 16:8.

9. 1 Pet 1:2.

10. 1 Cor 12:13; Acts 1:5, 8.

11. Acts 10:19; 16:7; John 14:16; 16:3.

12. 1 Cor 12; Rom 12:6f; Eph 4:11f.

13. John 15:16.

14. Isa 61:1. These three different classifications of individuals all have very specialized needs. Each ministry scenario will need to hear a different message.

15. Acts 1:8.

16. 1 Cor 13:1. Paul actually said that words not motivated by love were a clanging cymbal. I prefer, "noise."

17. Isa 61:2, 3.

18. Isa 61:3.

19. Isa 61:7.

healing and deliverance. It is also important to observe in Isaiah's prophecy the interrelatedness between receiving comfort and varying expressions of joy.[20] Because of Isaiah's threefold reference to joy (or celebration),[21] one can make a case that the ministry of worship is also to be a part of the mission of the church today.

We read further in Isaiah 61 that a part of the mission of the church is to rebuild forgotten and devastated municipalities.[22] This commonly neglected element of the mission of the church speaks to the biblical theme of justice. A wide range of ministry expressions is necessary to counter a multiplicity of injustices that run rampant in our society today. These varying ministry expressions were always meant to be a part of any church's mission.[23] The prophet juxtaposes the love that God has for those who practice justice,[24] and abhorrence for those who practice wrongdoing.[25] I have often stated to my students, "A Christian without a sense of justice in their life does not have blood running through their veins; all you have is just-ice." The church today should consider that the ills of society and culture are loudest in the very places where the church remains silent.

Still another aspect of the mission of the church is what Isaiah refers to as the calling of "priests of the Lord . . . ministers of our God."[26] This new leadership will be those who were among the imprisoned, broken, forgotten, impoverished, devastated and disgraced.[27] In short, God's new prophetic leadership will have little resemblance to what many churches look for in a leader. This part of the church's mission is what is referred to as spiritual leadership development, formation and discipleship.

And finally, Isaiah declares a culminating aspect of the mission of the church. As part of its mission, a church is to live in anticipation of the Lord's

20. Isa 61:3, 7, 11.

21. Ibid.

22. Isa 61:4.

23. Two examples of "justice ministries" on our campus at Lee University are our food pantry, where food is made available to our students that are in need; this same food pantry is organized to go out into low income neighborhoods surrounding our campus and distribute food every Saturday morning.

24. Isa 61:8a.

25. Isa 61:8b. And I would add that those who do nothing at all to speak out against flagrant injustices are just as wrong as those who are practicing things that break the heart of God.

26. Isa 61:6.

27. Isa 61:1–3.

radiant return. Isaiah states that God's people are to be like a bridegroom who awaits his bride.[28] Our Lord's return will signal the greatest worship experience, ever! God's people are to prepare themselves for Jesus' second coming by displaying a glorious outward countenance.[29] One ministry goal of the Apostle Paul was to do just this. Paul viewed his congregations as a bride, and his heart's desire was to prepare them in such a way that they would be (more than) ready for Jesus' return; a readiness much like a bride breathlessly prepares for her groom.[30] One might go so far as to say that Paul wanted to ignite his congregations for the ultimate worship celebration! Isaiah describes a person prepared for Christ as one who: is recognized by others, has been blessed by the Lord, has overwhelming joy, dons the robes of righteousness, and is described as a spring garden.[31] The above description is a bridal portrait of an individual who clearly has the Spirit of the sovereign Lord resting upon them. Further, this person has undergone a profound inner transformation by God's Spirit. These concluding verses of Isaiah 61 describe the results of three component factors of every church's mission. They are: the ministry of spiritual formation, the ministry of discipleship and the ministry of worship.

The above textual landscape of Isaiah 61 serves only to introduce several fundamental elements of what should be seen in the mission of any church. The above ideas are intended as a response to the opening question, "What is the mission of the church?" Introduced are the missional[32] ideas of Scripture, the Holy Spirit, calling, evangelism, discipleship, spiritual formation, worship, justice, culture, and context. Admittedly, the goal is to create in the reader an increased desire to read further. What lies ahead in the pages that follow is a showcase of each of these ideas through the individual voices of my colleagues. You will hear the voices of male and female, South African and North American, Pentecostal and Reformed, scholar and pastor, missiologist and educator. The contributors of the ensuing chapters are

---

28. Isa 61:10.

29. Isa 61:10; see also Rev 19:7–8.

30. 2 Cor 11:2.

31. Isa 61:9–11.

32. A proper understanding of missional begins with recovering a missionary understanding of God. This doctrine, known as *missio Dei*—the sending of God—views the church as the instrument of God's mission in the world. A missional church, or individual, is not sedentary. Every disciple is to be a sent agent of the kingdom of God, carrying the mission of God into every sphere of life. Missional Christ-followers are missionaries sent into all cultures, both Christ-professing and not. See Stott, "Living God," 3–9.

as diverse as one might imagine. Each voice is writing from years of experience and hearts that desire the church to become all that Jesus envisioned for it two thousand years ago.

Your reading will be a waste of time and effort if you do not apply this knowledge to the ministry and life setting where God has placed you. Read on, but turn your world upside down![33]

33. Acts 17:6.

The Primacy of Mission

Thomas J. Doolittle, PhD[1]

We are therefore Christ's ambassadors,
as though God were making his appeal through us.
We implore you on Christ's behalf: Be reconciled to God.

—2 Cor 5:20[2]

WHAT IS THE PURPOSE of the church? Why can't churches be more relevant? Why do we even need churches? These are questions that sting those of us who feel so passionate about the church and highly value its existence. Nevertheless, these are exactly the kind of questions being asked today, and we should be formulating some credible responses if we hope to pass our faith on to the coming generations. Today, many people have become disillusioned with churches to the point that they simply gave up and dropped out of church altogether. One such young man once wrote me the following note to explain his disenchantment with church.

1. Thomas J. Doolittle is Professor of Pastoral Ministries in the Department of Christian Ministries (DCM) at Lee University. While at Lee, he has served as the director for the Religion 200 program and as the chair of the DCM. Tom is an Ordained Bishop in the Church of God (Cleveland, TN). He joined the Lee University faculty in August 2003 after serving with his wife, Amy, in pastoral ministry for twenty-four years in Georgia, Alaska, and Kentucky. He received his PhD in Church and Community in 1996 from the Southern Baptist Theological Seminary in Louisville, KY. He served as co-editor and contributor for *Crossroads: Essays on a Christ-Centered Approach to Benevolence*. He also has presented at academic and church conferences and has written articles for church publications.

2. All Scripture quotations are from the New International Version (NIV) unless otherwise noted.

I look back on my Christianity and I see a boy with tons of faith who was always let down. I would pray and seek answers and guidance and would never get them. I would be assured of something in my "spirit" and that thing would not happen. I never felt the freedom and joy unspeakable and full of glory. Instead, I felt overwhelming guilt and shame for things that really aren't all that bad. To this day it has caused, I believe, an inferiority complex and a degree of self-loathing.

Unfortunately, this young man's tragic experience is not isolated. Far too many people have left church after similar disappointments and abuses. Still others leave because they think the church is no longer relevant or authentic. Now is the time for churches to rediscover their purpose so they can respond creatively to contemporary ministry challenges. To understand the purpose of the church, one should start with the founder of the church: Jesus (Matt 16:17–19). After Jesus was resurrected from the dead, he stayed with the disciples for forty days before he ascended to heaven. Just before he ascended, he imparted crucial instructions to the disciples regarding the continuance of his mission. In Matthew 28:18–20, Jesus issued the words that became the guiding force in all that the disciples did during their lifetimes. Today, we call this passage the Great Commission, and these words are still the fundamental guide for the church:

> Then Jesus came to them and said, "All authority in heaven and on earth has been given to me. Therefore go and make disciples of all nations, baptizing them in the name of the Father and of the Son and of the Holy Spirit, and teaching them to obey everything I have commanded you. And surely I am with you always, to the very end of the age." (Matt 28:18–20).

Commissioned by Jesus

The Great Commission, as declared by Jesus, provides the parameters for defining the mission of the church. These instructions by the Lord indicate the primacy of the mission for the very existence of the church. Jesus proclaimed that his universal authority undergirds his command to the church to make disciples who will "obey" all of his "commands." In this brief but powerful commission, Jesus established the purpose of the church, the process for fulfilling the mission, and the assurance of his presence to enable his followers to fulfill the Lord's directive.

It is obvious from the Lord's words that the mission the church is instructed to fulfill belongs to God, and the church is called to join God in fulfilling his mission. The mission is often described as the *missio Dei*, or the mission of God. This phrase indicates that the ownership of the mission belongs to God, and the church has been entrusted through Christ to devote themselves to God's mission. The Great Commission provides the basic parameters for guiding the church in maintaining focus and purpose in its functions, ministries, and worship. Everything the church does should reflect the *missio Dei* that Jesus delivered to the church.

The Missional God

The concept of *missio Dei* includes the recognition that God has been actively engaged in the world for redemptive purposes since the transgressions of Adam and Eve. Jesus clearly proclaimed the *missio Dei*, and the Holy Spirit empowered the church to continue God's mission in the world. At the heart of God's mission is his love for all people and his engagement with his creation and with all cultures.[3] God is the principle actor in the *missio Dei*, and the church joins with God to proclaim the gospel of Jesus Christ, calling all people to reconciliation with God.

The *missio Dei* includes the emphasis that mission proceeds from God's nature and, as such, relates to the doctrine of the Trinity. Thus, as God the Father sends the Son into the world for mission, and the Father and the Son send the Holy Spirit, the mission is expanded by the Father, Son, and Spirit as the Trinity commissioning the church to continue its mission in the world.[4] God is the principle actor for *missio Dei*; not congregations, denominations, or parachurch ministries. Through Jesus Christ, God provided redemption for all of his creation that extends to individuals and to all things God created. The church joins in the *missio Dei* by proclaiming Jesus as Redeemer, declaring his works of redemption, and calling the world to reconciliation in Christ. To be truly missional, the church must be sensitive and obedient to the leadership of the Holy Spirit, the third person of the Trinity.[5] Therefore, the church is called to join God in fulfilling his mission to reconcile the world to himself.

3. Bosch, *Transforming Mission*, 10.
4. Bosch, *Transforming Mission*, 390.
5. Van Gelder, *Ministry of the Missional Church*, 19.

The Missional Church

Churches who adopt the *missio Dei* as the guiding theme of their congregational practices and ministries are often described as missional churches. A missional church or ministry will embrace *missio Dei* as its purpose for existence, recognizing God's ownership of the mission and their responsibility to be faithful to their missional calling. God is the one who sets the priorities for mission, and missional churches embrace God's mission as described in his word and as led by the Holy Spirit, rejecting the temptation to let personal preferences become the criteria for ministry development. Since the *missio Dei* concerns all creation, missional churches also concern themselves with biblical stewardship of resources, the environment, and all living creatures. The mission of God has been revealed through the life, works, and words of Jesus Christ, and the church is called and empowered by the Holy Spirit to continue God's mission until "then end of the age" (Matt 28:20b).

Congregations and parachurch organizations which adopt a missional approach to ministry emphasize that God cares about the holistic needs of people. God's concern and care extends to the whole person, body and spirit, and includes the spiritual and physical needs of all people. Too often, the church emphasizes concern for the spiritual needs of people, while neglecting emotional and physical concerns. However, Jesus was obviously concerned for both. In his first sermon, he asserted that he had come to heal and deliver people from spiritual and physical sufferings through the power of the Spirit (Luke 4:18–19).

The Missional Jesus

The Sermon on the Mount is replete with instructions that impact the spiritual and physical well-being of those listening to Jesus. A simple cursory review of the sermon in Matthew 5–7 reveals that Jesus is concerned about our personal salvation (Matt 5:3, 6, 16, 19), relationships with others (5:9, 22–24), personal morality (5:27–32), almsgiving (6:1–4), prayer life (6:5–15), priorities (6:19–21, 24), daily provisions (6:11, 26, 30, 33), quality of life (7–11), and spiritual fruit-bearing (7:17–21). The Sermon on the Mount illustrates how our spiritual and physical needs are so closely connected.

Since Jesus was so concerned about all aspects of people's lives, then the church should be also. In Matthew 25:31–46, Jesus' poignant parable

4

of the sheep and goats illustrates the relationship between the spiritual and physical aspects of our lives. In this parable, the sheep are "blessed" and "inherit the kingdom" because they have ministered to the physical needs of others (vv. 34–36). In stark contrast with the sheep, the goats receive a daunting indictment for their severe neglect of the physical concerns of suffering people (vv. 41–46). This parable establishes the priority God gives to caring for those suffering around us, and demonstrates the expectancies God places upon believers for caring for the holistic needs of others. The reason for this emphasis is revealed by Jesus' assertion that whatever we have done or not done for those in such obvious need, we "have done it unto" him (Matt 25:40, 45).

Churches who are missional in focus strive for balance in their congregational ministries. It is not uncommon for congregations to emphasize their ministry priorities based on traditions, personal preferences, denominational emphases, or even convenience. For example, some mainline churches may emphasize social justice or benevolence care, whereas some evangelical churches may focus on evangelism or discipleship. A missional congregation will seek balance in ministry, allotting appropriate energies and resources for the whole mission of God, including biblical justice, benevolent action, discipleship, and evangelism.

Missional Discipleship

A central theme that runs through missional churches is radical discipleship based on the mission of God that was revealed through Jesus and declared by Christ in the Great Commission. Evangelism is critical to the church's mandate in the *missio Dei*, just as it was in Jesus' own ministry (Luke 19:10; Matt 20:28). Nevertheless, Jesus was not interested in just gaining converts; he came to build his church, which requires evangelism and transformational discipleship.[6] Evangelism without radical discipleship will fail to impact communities and the world in ways that will bring about justice, benevolence, and liberation from oppression. Discipleship without evangelism cannot liberate people from sin and provide them with eternal life (Rom 3:23; 6:23).

The missional church recognizes that many people are dissatisfied with churches today, and that large numbers of young people are giving up altogether. Some of the discontent is related to perceptions that the church

6. Greenway, "Confronting Urban Contexts," 45.

is not relevant or may not be authentic. Non-missional churches who focus primarily on evangelism may think that social justice or benevolence may distract the congregation from their primary purpose. For a missional-minded church, this is not the case at all. Instead, missional churches will proclaim the gospel of Christ while seeking to engage in biblical justice and lifestyles that exemplify the truth of their message. Such biblical justice actions can help create a bridge of trust with the community, which can enhance missional endeavors and others' perceptions of the church.[7] The rebuilding of trust through holistic ministries can contribute to the evangelistic efforts of churches. Indeed, the church may not even be able to "witness credibly to or participate effectively in God's mission without faithful discipleship" that includes missional concepts.[8]

Characteristics of Missional Churches

Michael Frost developed an evaluation instrument for denominational consulting in which he described three characteristics of a missional congregation. Frost's description presents an approach to missional ministry that balances the proclamation of the gospel with Christian living that demonstrates the reign of God, which is a crucial concept in many missional church models.[9] First, a missional church proclaims God's reign through Christ. Next, it manifests the reign of Christ through holistic ministry and actions. Finally, the church exemplifies God's mission in various ways that reflect priorities based on the interpretation and application of Jesus' life and ministry.[10] Frost expands each of the items to provide criteria for determining if a particular congregation is missional.

Many writers such as Frost have sought to describe missional churches in an effort to provide clarifying descriptions or even evaluative criteria. This has proven to be a difficult challenge that has not provided a singular understanding of what constitutes a missional church. However, there are a number of themes that are threaded through much of the literature on missional churches. These themes may provide a basic outline for the characteristics of a missional church. Whereas there are numerous such themes, here I will briefly discuss five common characteristics of missional

7. Carrasco, "A Pound of Justice," 251.

8. Van Gelder and Zscheile, *Missional Church in Perspective*, 148.

9. Frost, *Road to Missional*, 60.

10. Frost, *Road to Missional*, 61–62.

churches found in the United States. It should be noted that some missional themes will be further developed in other chapters in this text. Many of these themes are not unique to missional churches. However, missional churches seek to incorporate such missional themes throughout all aspects of their congregational lives and ministries.

Mission-Minded

Missional churches and leaders recognize that the host culture is post-Christian and postmodern. Pluralism has become commonplace, especially in urban areas or even the suburbs of major cities. In many places, the social landscape is no longer friendly for churches and avid Christ-followers. Thus, missional churches train their members to become missionaries to their communities and then send them out to fulfill the Great Commission.[11]

Rather than seeking only to attract non-Christians to church services or special events, missional congregations focus on sending their people out into the community where the unchurched folks live, work, and gather. They become true ambassadors of Christ: "We are therefore Christ's ambassadors, as though God were making his appeal through us. We implore you on Christ's behalf: Be reconciled to God" (2 Cor 5:20).

Christ-Centered

The missional church emphasizes that Jesus Christ is the main purpose for their existence. Too often, the mission of the church seems to be more about programs or agendas than it is about Christ and people. The primary purpose of the church is revealed in the message of the gospel: "For God so loved the world that he gave his one and only Son, that whoever believes in him shall not perish but have eternal life" (John 3:16). God's love for all people is a guiding force in missional churches, and becomes the primary motivating factor for their ministries as they seek to truly love their neighbors as God loves them (Matt 22:37–40).

Many people today are disenchanted with the church because they think the church is not interested in them or is not relevant. Interestingly, many unchurched people, especially the "emerging generations" who do not like traditional church formats, have a sincere interest in knowing more

11. Driscoll, *Confessions of a Reformission Rev*, 20.

about Jesus and his teachings.[12] Missional churches refocus their resources and ministries so that Jesus is at the center of everything they do, so his love will be manifested throughout the life of the church. To do this may require that churches be "recalibrated" around Jesus, the founder of the church, to reclaim "the centrality of Jesus for the faith and thought."[13]

Kingdom-Oriented

Many of the traditional models of ministry emphasize programs or seeker-friendly approaches to ministry that may seem too limited or inauthentic to unchurched people. One problem with such approaches is that congregations may become too narrow or overly departmentalized. This can lead to a "silo mentality that reduces Jesus' mission to a department" within a particular church.[14] Kingdom-oriented churches declare Jesus' reign as Lord and Savior through proclamation, worship, service, ministries, and lifestyles that exemplify and communicate the gospel in ways unreached and un-churched people can understand.

By emphasizing the kingdom of God and the reign of Christ, the mission of the church is unified and not limited to artificial silos of ministry territories. Ministry is focused on the reign of Christ and reaching unchurched people with the good news of Christ. The church emphasizes the need to engage locally and globally in ministries that reflect the principles of God's kingdom. Kingdom-oriented churches pray and work for the fulfillment of the Lord's Prayer: "Our Father in heaven, hallowed be your name, your kingdom come, your will be done, on earth as it is in heaven" (Matthew 6:9–10).

Spirit-Directed

Missional churches seek to be Spirit-directed in all aspects of their congregational life and ministries. The church joins in the *missio Dei* with a Spirit-consciousness so they can be sensitive to the leadership of the Holy Spirit and follow his direction.[15] Missional churches and their leaders are

---

12. Kimball, *They Like Jesus*, 11.

13. Frost and Hirsch, *ReJesus*, 167.

14. Wegner and Magruder, *Missional Moves*, 49.

15. Van Gelder, *Ministry of the Missional Church*, 19.

consistently seeking to discover what the Spirit is doing in the community and how they may join in his work for the kingdom of God. They know that the Holy Spirit is already at work in their communities and throughout the world, and they desire to join him in the *missio Dei*.

When Jesus launched his public ministry, he declared that Spirit of God had anointed him and empowered him for the works he would do (Luke 4:16–21). Missional churches and leaders emphasize their own reliance on the Holy Spirit for fulfilling the calling of God. Jesus told his disciples that they needed the Spirit for the challenges ahead and instructed them to receive the Holy Spirit (Luke 24:49; John 20:22; Acts 1:8; 2:1–4). Thus, the Spirit of God set forth the church on its mission, indicating that the mission will always be the mission of the Holy Spirit.[16] Today, the church still needs the empowerment of the Spirit, just as the early church did. Missional churches gladly acknowledge their dependency on the Holy Spirit and welcome his leadership in the fulfilling God's mission.

Culturally Engaged

One of the most challenging aspects of being missional concerns the area of cultural engagement. Throughout its existence, the church has struggled to find the proper relationship with culture. Sometimes the responses of churches gravitate toward the extremes. For example, some churches may contend that culture is sinful and their members must withdraw from much of culture if they are true believers, whereas other churches may strive to relate to culture so much that they lose their identities through cultural accommodation.

Missional churches seek to find a healthy, effective balance for developing ministries that are culturally relevant while challenging the culture with the gospel of Christ. Thus, missional churches and leaders seek creative ways to minister and proclaim the gospel while calling people to accept Christ as Lord and Savior. Churches that seek to engage their cultural contexts are willing to take risks and to try new approaches to ministry. They are not afraid of making mistakes, being flexible to change directions as the Holy Spirit guides them in kingdom service. The apostle Paul faced similar challenges as he labored industriously to proclaim the gospel throughout the Roman Empire. When he preached in Athens at the Areopagus, Paul quoted from the Athenians' own poets to engage

---

16. Newbigin, *Open Secret*, 58.

their culture, and then challenged them by proclaiming Christ's resurrection as God's call to reconciliation (Acts 17:22–34). Paul's missional methodology, as recorded in Acts and in the Pauline epistles, provides stimulating insights for engaging culture with the gospel of Christ. This is the passion of missional churches.

Conclusion

We live in uncertain times that present new challenges and opportunities for churches to try new ways of reaching people with the gospel of Christ. As the church moves forward with creative and contemporary ministries, we also must remember our faith foundations. The best way to do this is to keep Jesus as the center of the church. He presents to us the perfect model for reaching those who are lost, developing true disciples, building the church, and engaging cultures with the gospel. The apostle Paul cautioned Timothy to "Remember Jesus Christ, raised from the dead, descended from David. This is my gospel" (2 Tim 2:8). Obviously, Paul believed that these words would serve to guide Timothy in his role as pastor. We too must remember Jesus as we serve as ministry leaders in churches, non-profits, or parachurch organizations, whether near home or abroad. We are Christ's ambassadors and missionaries, calling the world to be reconciled to him. This is the mission of the church!

Questions for Reflection

1. How does the Great Commission relate to the primacy of mission for the church?

2. Why should the church join in the *missio Dei*?

3. Why is radical discipleship crucial for fulfilling the mission of the church?

4. What are the five characteristics of missional churches? Summarize each in one sentence.

For Further Reading

Bosch, David J. *Transforming Mission: Paradigm Shifts in Theology of Mission*. Maryknoll, NY: Orbis, 1991.

Frost, Michael. *The Road to Missional: Journey to the Center of the Church*. Grand Rapids: Baker, 2011.

Kimball, Dan. *They Like Jesus but Not the Church: Insights from Emerging Generations*. Grand Rapids: Zondervan, 2007.

Newbigin, Leslie. *The Open Secret: An Introduction to the Theology of Mission*. Grand Rapids: Eerdmans, 1995.

Van Gelder, Craig. *The Ministry of the Missional Church: A Community Led by the Spirit*. Grand Rapids: Baker, 2007.

Ott, Craig, Ed. *The Mission of the Church: Five Views in Conversation*. Grand Rapids: Baker Academic, 2016.

Roxburgh, Alan J. *Structured for Mission: Renewing the Culture of the Church*. Downers Grove, IL: InterVarsity, 2015.

The Centrality of Scripture

John A. Lombard Jr., DMin[1]

All scripture is inspired by God
and is useful for teaching, for reproof,
for correction, and for training in righteousness,
so that everyone who belongs to God may be proficient,
equipped for every good work.

—2 TIM 3:16–17 (NRSV)

"I DON'T CARE WHAT the Scripture says, I know what I experienced."
"I don't know what the Scripture says, I know what my tradition teaches."
"By reason alone I determine truth."

These statements show us the urgency in establishing the place of Scripture in the life of the Church. The Scripture is also called the Scriptures, the word of God, the word, Sacred Writings and the Bible. These terms refer to the Christian Scriptures or biblical canon, thirty-nine books in the Old Testament and twenty-seven books in the New Testament. These designations will be used interchangeably in this chapter.

---

1. John A. Lombard Jr. serves as an Adjunct faculty member both at Lee University's Department of Christian Ministries and the Pentecostal Theological Seminary. He holds a DMin from Vanderbilt University. His practical ministry experiences include: continual pastoring since 1966, Coordinator of the Church of God Ministerial Internship Program in Tennessee since 1980, Church of God Tennessee State Council (20 years), and Church of God Ministerial Licensing Board. He is the author of a variety of periodical articles and book chapters. He wrote *Speaking for God*, and co-authored *Speaking in Tongues: Initial Evidence of Spirit Baptism?* and *Spiritual Gifts For Today? For Me?* He and his wife, Diana, have three children and six grandchildren.

There are some who do not use the Bible and the word of God as synonymous terms. Some of these believe that the Bible *contains* the word of God. With this understanding, the myths have to be removed and various criticisms employed in order to discover the kernel of truth. This is a subjective approach. A reaction to this approach says that the Bible becomes the word of God. According to this, when the Bible connects with someone in a personal encounter, at that moment it becomes the word of God. This approach contends that the Bible becomes the word of God only as proclaimed and received at certain critical moments. The view held by the author of this chapter is that the Bible is the word of God. The word is not dependent upon certain criticisms, such as form criticism or redaction criticism. The word is also not dependent upon connecting with someone personally. So, the Bible does not merely contain the word of God, nor does it at certain points become the word of God. Rather, it is the word of God. This issue has fuller treatment later in this chapter.

The Scripture is God's Revelation

The Scripture is not merely a compilation of human stories or mythologies which attempt to explain God and human existence. Nature reveals that there is a Supreme Being (Rom 1:20), but special revelation is needed to know about the attributes or characteristics of this Supreme Being and about the relationship this One has with the ones whom the Supreme Being has created. God has chosen to give us further revelation. God progressively revealed God's nature and desires through personal encounters, divinely-sent messengers, and catastrophic events. God chose Israel to receive, contain, and share special revelation and the Divine Covenant. Through the Old Covenant, God prepared the world for the definitive and ultimate revelation, God's Son, Jesus Christ (Heb 1:1–4). God chose to give us a record of this revelation by inspiring, superintending, and guiding human beings: "Because no prophecy ever came by human will, but men and women moved by the Holy Spirit spoke from God" (2 Pet 1:21, NRSV); "All Scripture is God-breathed" (2 Tim 3:16a).[2] God enhanced the thinking and spiritual perception of the human authors so that, through their personalities, backgrounds and vocabularies, the exact words were chosen to give God's revelation.

2. All Scripture quotations are from the New International Version (NIV) unless otherwise noted.

The Scripture is Synonymous with the Bible and the Word of God

In order to assert the centrality of Scripture, it is important to consider some of the reasons the Bible is viewed as Scripture, the very word of God. On what basis can it be said that the terms Scripture, Bible, and word of God can be used interchangeably?

Unity in Diversity

The sixty-six books which met the standards set forth to be included in the biblical canon were written by about forty authors over a period of 1400–1500 years. There were many differences in their backgrounds, circumstances, and approaches. With the diversity, a tremendous unity prevails as God guided them to move the story along from creation to consummation. Throughout, there is consistency in the revelation of the nature of God and God's relationship to God's people and world.

The Testimony of Jesus

How did Jesus view the Scripture?

Defense against Satan

When Satan brought his full attack against Jesus in the wilderness temptations, Jesus quoted the word of God. He did not argue, but he relied upon the power of God's word to withstand the attack.

Permanent Truth

Jesus prefaced his Scripture quotation during Satan's attack with "It is written" (Matt 4:4). It could be translated "It *stands* written." God's word is established by God's very nature, which does not change. Jesus' statement underscores Isaiah 40:8: "The grass withers and the flower fades but the Word of the Lord stands forever." Jesus commented on his own message: "Heaven and earth will pass away, but my words will never pass away" (Matt 24:35).

Prophetic of Himself

Jesus challenged the Jews, "You study the Scriptures diligently because you think that in them you have eternal life. These are the very Scriptures that testify about me" (John 5:39). These Jews are the ones who claimed the Scriptures to be authoritative, and they boasted concerning their knowledge of Scripture, but they denied that Jesus had a unique relationship to the Father and that he was equal to the Father. Jesus stated unequivocally that the Scriptures bear witness to him. After his resurrection, Jesus shared the following with two of his disciples on the road to Emmaus: "And beginning with Moses and all the Prophets, he explained to them what was said in all the Scriptures concerning himself" (Luke 24:27). These two disciples knew the Scriptures, but they had not grasped their meaning. Jesus showed them from the Scriptures many things that had been predicted concerning the Messiah and which were being fulfilled in him. These things included the necessity of the crucifixion and the inevitability of the resurrection.

Sufficient to Generate Faith

In Luke 16, Jesus presents a discussion between the rich man in the torments of hell and Abraham, who is with Lazarus in a place of blessedness. The rich man begs that Lazarus be sent back to warn his five brothers so that they will not go to the place of torments. The reply is, "They have Moses and the Prophets; let them listen to them." "No," the rich man says, "but if someone from the dead goes to them, they will repent." The emphatic reply is, "If they do not listen to Moses and the Prophets, they will not be convinced even if someone rises from the dead" (Luke 16:29–31). The Scripture (Moses and the Prophets) is sufficient to generate faith. If the Scripture does not produce faith, nothing else will.

Completely Reliable

Jesus requested the Father concerning his disciples, "Sanctify them by the truth; your word is truth" (John 17:17). Jesus accepted the word of God as absolute, complete truth. He further stated, "It is easier for heaven and earth to disappear than for the least stroke of a pen to drop out of the Law" (Luke 16:17). God watches over the word of God to perform it. It is completely reliable.

15

Fulfilled Prophecy

The Scripture includes foretelling of future events. There is historical evidence that many of these prophecies have already been fulfilled. Jesus said, "The Scriptures must be fulfilled" (Mark 14:49b). Matthew shows that many things happened in order that the Scriptures might be fulfilled. He often uses the clause, "that it might be fulfilled." The prophecies and fulfillments included the virgin birth (Matt 1:20–23); Mary, Joseph, and Jesus' travel to Egypt (2:15); Jesus' dwelling in Nazareth (2:23); Jesus' casting out of demons and healing (8:16–17); and others.

The late Dr. Charles Beach was a professor at Lee University. He also was an adjunct professor at the University of Tennessee. As a guest lecturer in a Personal Evangelism class that I taught, Dr. Beach emphasized fulfilled prophecy to show that the Bible is trustworthy. He had asked a mathematics professor at the university to calculate the odds against Old Testament prophecies being fulfilled. Dr. Beach reported that of fifty-five prophecies in Isaiah about Jesus which have been fulfilled, the odds were 36,028,797,018,963,968 to one; that is, over thirty-six quadrillion to one against their being fulfilled. Dr. Beach also reported that, of 332 prophecies in the Old Testament about Jesus which have already been fulfilled, the odds were eight million trigintillion to one against their being fulfilled. This evidence indicates the reliability of the Bible, and that a divine mind guided the human authors.[3]

The Power of the Bible to Change Lives

God uses divine revelation to be the instrument of change in individuals' lives. The word convicts, cleanses, and connects people to God. A young man in China was reluctantly given permission to check out a copy of the Bible from the library for two weeks. Because of Shakespeare's references to the Bible, the young man, an atheist, just wanted to become acquainted with it. As he read the Bible, he became convinced of the reality of God, aware of his own sinfulness, and persuaded of the provisions of Jesus Christ for salvation. His life was changed by God as he read the word of God. Paul said, "For I am not ashamed of the gospel, because it is the power of God that brings salvation to everyone who believes" (Rom 1:16a).

3. Beach, "Is the Bible Really True?"

Equating New Testament Writings with Old Testament Scripture

The apostles of Jesus had a high view of Scripture. It is therefore significant what Peter said of Paul's writings. Speaking of Paul's letters, Peter said, "His letters contain some things that are hard to understand, which ignorant and unstable people distort, as they do the other Scriptures, to their own destruction" (2 Pet 3:16b). Peter affirms that Paul's letters are Scriptures, even as are the other Scriptures.

Paul himself affirms that what the believers at Thessalonica heard was the word of God. He says, "We also constantly give thanks to God for this, that when you received the Word of God that you heard from us, you accepted it not as a human word but as what it really is, God's Word, which is also at work in you believers" (1 Thess 2:13, NRSV).

The Scripture Establishes the Teaching of the Church

"All Scripture is God-breathed and is useful for teaching" (2 Tim 3:16a). Note 1 Corinthians 15:3–4: "For what I received I passed on to you as of first importance: that Christ died for our sins according to the Scriptures, that He was buried, that He was raised on the third day according to the Scriptures, and that he appeared to Cephas [Peter], and then to the Twelve." These verses indicate that the teaching (doctrine) of the church is not human conjecture, not human opinion, not merely human tradition, but it is based on the Scripture.

There are basically four ways truth is discerned, and the teachings are set forth: reason, emotional experience, church councils/tradition, and the Christian Scripture. Each of these has a role to fill, but the centrality of Scripture must be emphasized here. "Centrality" means primary importance or essential significance. Scripture alone establishes the teachings of the church. The Scripture judges the church. The decisions of the councils, such as the Council of Nicea (AD 325), as well as the tradition of the church, must be judged by the Scriptures. A person who says, "I don't know what the Scripture says, I know what my tradition teaches," makes tradition central and not the Scripture. The Scripture validates or invalidates personal experiences. A person who says, "I don't care what the Scripture says, I know what I have experienced," puts experience central. The Scripture takes precedence over reason. A person who says, "By reason alone I determine truth" negates the centrality of Scripture. Some things the human mind cannot grasp. For example, who by reason can understand an eternal God; who by reason can comprehend eternal life or eternal separation from God? These truths are taught by Scripture, so they are received whether the human mind can or cannot grasp them. Let reason, experience, and tradition be examined and judged by the word of God.

Paul told Timothy, "What you have heard from me, keep as the pattern of sound teaching, with faith and love in Christ Jesus. Guard the good deposit that was entrusted to you—guard it with the help of the Holy Spirit who lives in us" (2 Tim 1:13–14). Paul had given Timothy the "very Word of God," and he urges Timothy to guard the deposit of truth and keep it as the pattern of sound teaching. Paul states further, "But as for you, continue in what you have learned and have become convinced of, because you know those from whom you learned it, and how from infancy you have known the Holy Scriptures, which are able to make you wise for salvation through faith in Christ Jesus" (2 Tim 3:14–15). Jude urged Christian believers to "Contend for the faith that was once for all entrusted to God's holy people" (Jude 3b). "The faith" was the body of teaching entrusted to believers. It was "once for all" entrusted, which means that it is established; it does not change. Jude was constrained by the Holy Spirit, the Spirit of Truth, to appeal to believers to be aggressive in preserving the teaching established by the Scriptures. The Scripture establishes the teaching of the church.

The Scripture Guides the Church (the People of God) in Righteous Living

"All Scripture is God-breathed and is useful for teaching, rebuking, correcting and training in righteousness" (2 Tim 3:16). The Scripture is of primary importance in instructing the people of God in how to live. The word first penetrates the depths of our being to discern not only our behavior but also our motives and intentions. "For the word of God is alive and active. Sharper than any double-edged sword, it penetrates even to dividing soul and spirit, joints and marrow; it judges the thoughts and attitudes of the heart" (Heb 4:12). The word of God brings reproof and correction. It instructs us concerning repentance and reconciliation. It then offers guidance in continuing to live in accordance with God's will. "How can a young person stay on the path of purity? By living according to your word" (Ps 119:9). The Scripture then gives encouragement—"For everything that was written in the past was written to teach us, so that through the endurance taught in the Scriptures and the encouragement they provide we might have hope" (Rom 15:4).

Righteous living is living in right standing with God and other human beings. The Scripture exhorts the believer to accept the new creation one has become with its new possibilities and, by faith, actualize or bring into reality those possibilities. The Scripture shows the divine resources available to the believer. The Scripture proclaims that authentic Christian character is a work of divine grace and a production of the Holy Spirit (Gal 5:22–23). Christian character exercises freedom with responsibility, without partiality, and without prejudices. The "one another" passages in the Bible guide how fellow believers should relate to each other. With humility and submission to God, the believer lives with confidence as a "super-conqueror" (Rom 8:37). With the guidance of Scripture, the believer exercises spiritual discernment (righteous judgment) and engages effectively in spiritual warfare.

The Scripture Equips the People of God for their Work

"All Scripture is inspired by God. . .so that everyone who belongs to God may be proficient, equipped for every good work" (2 Tim 3:16a, 17, NRSV). Proficiency, the ability to go forward and accomplish, comes from training and practice. The word of God provides training in righteousness.

The Christian is created to be God's workmanship, God's work of art, God's masterpiece, or God's handiwork. The word used here for "God's masterpiece" is *Poiema* (ποίημα). The believer is "created in Christ Jesus to do good works, which God prepared in advance for us to do" (Eph 2:10). The Scripture indicates that each person in the body of Christ has a unique place to fill and work to do in partnership with others in the body.

Jesus said, "As the Father has sent me, I am sending you" (John 20:21b). The work of believers is a continuation of the work which Jesus did while upon the Earth in body. As Jesus ministered in the power of the Holy Spirit, it is also imperative that believers live and work in the power of the Holy Spirit. The Scripture enlightens us concerning the baptism in the Holy Spirit, as well as gifts administered by the Holy Spirit.

The Scripture offers encouragement and hope to the believer: "Therefore, my beloved, be steadfast, immoveable, always excelling in the work of the Lord, because you know that in the Lord your labor is not in vain" (1 Cor 15:58, NRSV).

As he neared death, Paul expressed his hope and the hope of all believers: "I have fought the good fight, I have finished the race, I have kept the faith. From now on there is reserved for me the crown of righteousness, which the Lord, the righteous judge, will give me on that day, and not only to me but also to all who have longed for his appearing" (2 Tim 4:7–8, NRSV).

So, the Scripture equips the believers to fulfill the unique work to which God calls and equips them. Whatever they do, the believers are to do everything for the glory of God (1 Cor 10:31). Whatever they do in word or work, they are to do everything in the name of the Lord Jesus with a heart of thankfulness to God (Col 3:17). To do everything in the name of the Lord Jesus is to do all in his authority, according to his commandments and in the power of his provisions.

The Scripture is the Church's Proclamation

Proclamation includes preaching, teaching, and evangelizing. What message does the church proclaim? What hope can the church offer in the place of hopelessness? What peace can the church offer to persons with internal turmoil? Merely describing the problems does not solve them. Merely identifying with the downtrodden and marginalized does not lift them. The church has a unique place in the world. Its proclamation is a dynamic life-changing and life-giving message, the good news of the Scripture. Jesus set the pattern. When he entered Capernaum, the people filled the house where he was and Jesus "preached the word to them" (Mark 2:2b). The early believers followed this pattern. When believers were persecuted and, except for the apostles, they were driven from Jerusalem, "those who had been scattered preached the word wherever they went" (Acts 8:4).

A solemn charge is given in the Scripture: "Preach the word; be prepared in season and out of season; correct, rebuke and encourage—with great patience and careful instruction" (2 Tim 4:2). The word of God reveals the heinousness of sin and the tremendous magnitude of divine grace. The proclaimed word produces and increases faith (Rom 10:17). The gospel (God's good news) communicates God's power that brings salvation (Rom 1:16). God's word softens and purifies hard hearts (Jer 23:28–29). When faced with challenges and other important work, the apostles said, "But we will devote ourselves to prayer and to the ministry of the word" (Acts 6:4,

NASB). Their commitment shows the centrality of the word of God. The Bible is the book of the church. True believers embrace it, practice it, and proclaim it.

Conclusion

The message of the church is determined by the Scripture. The mission of the church is defined and described by the Scripture. The lifestyle of the believer is prescribed and enabled by the Scripture. The future of the church is revealed by the Scripture. Scripture is central, essential, and of primary importance in the life of the Christian believer and in the life of the Church.

Questions for Reflection

1. In what way is Scripture central in determining truth?

2. How would you describe Jesus' understanding of Scripture?

3. How does fulfilled prophecy demonstrate the validity of Scripture?

4. By saying that some distort Paul's writing, as they do "the other Scriptures," what does Peter reveal about his understanding of Paul's writing?

5. Why is special revelation needed, even though there is natural revelation?

6. State three ways the Scriptures benefit the believer.

For Further Reading

Carson, D. A. *The Enduring Authority of the Christian Scriptures.* Grand Rapids: Eerdmans, 2016.

Clark, Gordon H. *The Concept of Biblical Authority.* Phillipsburg, NJ: Presbyterian & Reformed, 1980.

Geisler, Norman L., and Ronald M. Brooks. *When Skeptics Ask.* Grand Rapids: Baker, 1996.

McDowell, Josh. *The New Evidence That Demands a Verdict.* Nashville, TN: Nelson, 1999.

Rogers, Jack, ed. *A Revival of Biblical Authority.* Waco, Texas: Word, 1977.

Wright, N. T. *Scripture and the Authority of God: How to Read the Bible Today.* New York: HarperOne, 2011.

The Indispensability of the Spirit

Terry L. Cross, PhD[1]

The Spirit of the Lord is on me,
because he has anointed me to preach
good news to the poor.
He has sent me to proclaim freedom
for the prisoners and recovery of sight for the blind,
to release the oppressed, to proclaim the year of the Lord's favor.

—LUKE 4:18–19[2]

TO DESCRIBE THE HOLY Spirit as indispensable to the mission of the church is to state the obvious. Indeed, it is so obvious that one may wonder why we should offer a chapter on this topic. We humans have a way of knowing something with our minds, yet gradually ignoring it with our lives. Anyone who has worked in the church has encountered this very human problem.

---

1. Terry L. Cross, PhD, is the Dean of the School of Religion and Professor of Systematic Theology at Lee University. Cross has pastored for twelve years in Ohio, New Jersey, and Connecticut. His education has been from Lee College (BA), Ashland Theological Seminary in Ohio (MA, MDiv), and Princeton Theological Seminary (ThM, PhD). From the latter school, he received the PhD in Systematic Theology, focusing on the Doctrine of God in the theology of Karl Barth. He has written several books (one on Karl Barth's use of dialectic and one on calling and vocation), and is currently writing a two-volume work on ecclesiology from a Pentecostal perspective. He is also working on a multi-volume *History of Christian Doctrines*. Cross is married to Linda, and they have one daughter, Tara, who is married to Kevin Snider, and one grandchild, Luke.

2. All Scripture quotations are from the New International Version (NIV) unless otherwise noted.

We start with a clear reliance on the action of God's Spirit in our midst and gradually lose sight of the need for that divine action; the result is usually an enhanced focus on our own abilities and strengths to perform the job. We shift from "look what God has wrought" to "look what I have brought." In this chapter, I will provide a theological rationale for the necessity of the Spirit's presence and activity in any effective ministry endeavor of the church. Woven together with this theological rationale will be practical steps on how to cooperate with the Spirit in our lives and ministry together within the Christian church.

The Nature of the Holy Spirit

It is important to begin our reflection with an understanding of the nature of the Spirit. Who is the Spirit? Perhaps it is best to first consider who the Spirit is not. The Spirit is not an impersonal force or some lifeless instrument in the hands of a personal God. The Spirit is not the same as the human spirit. The Spirit is not a created angel given special powers by God. As ancient Christian teaching has established, the Holy Spirit is the Lord and Giver of Life—no less God than is God the Father or God the Son. It was the Spirit who established order out of chaos during creation (Gen 1:2); it was the Spirit who enabled the prophets and holy people of old to speak on God's behalf as they were "moved along" by the Spirit (2 Pet 1:21); it was the Spirit who overshadowed Mary and brought about the conception of the Incarnate Son of God (Luke 1:35); it was the Spirit who guided Jesus' own ministry, and who still guides the church today.

A great missionary theologian of the twentieth century, Lesslie Newbigin, has reminded us that we cannot understand the church's mission without understanding the doctrine of the Triune God.[3] Why is this the case? First, it is the Triune God who coordinates and executes the eternal plan of God. Second, each person of the Trinity leads a particular aspect of the *missio Dei* (the mission of God). God the Father coordinates and oversees the eternal plan; God the Son executes it in the reality of human existence through the incarnation; and God the Spirit applies the eternal plan within human lives, as well as assures the goal of summing up all things in Christ (1 Cor 15:22–28).[4] All work together in perfect unity.

3. Newbigin, *Trinitarian Doctrine*, 82.

4. On this point, compare the excellent work of Jürgen Moltmann on the "future of the Son" in *Trinity and the Kingdom*, 91–92.

Unfortunately, many Christians have a naïve, unreflective view of the Trinity. While it is impossible to give adequate context for understanding the Trinity in this brief chapter, it would create a grave misunderstanding if the nature of the Spirit were discussed without any reference to this mystery of the faith. Many Christians conceive of the Trinity in very physical terms—like an egg (the shell, yolk, and white), three parts yet one egg. This first-grade level of Trinitarian understanding is frequently the extent of believers' meditation on this mystery of the nature of the Godhead. The Trinity is much more than three parts rolled into one entity. Indeed, there is no ready-made analogy for the Trinity in our physical world; there is nothing like the Trinity among humankind or even in our loftiest imaginations. Our God is far above our ability to encompass or control with our minds.

So if the Trinity is beyond human comprehension, why should we discuss it? The fact that God has revealed himself as One God, yet with three dimensions, points us toward seeking further understanding of this aspect of our faith. We discuss it because God has shown himself to exist as One yet Three—as Three yet One. It is the nature of the God who encounters us to be Triune. Moreover, studying the doctrine of the Trinity provides Christians a basis for reflecting on how God interacts as Father, Son, and Spirit within perfect unity that is also marked by difference. This opens the way for understanding our mission in the world through the nature of our God. Christians are not monotheists in the most radical sense of that term; that is, we do not worship a single, unmoving unit we call "god." Christians are also not polytheists in any sense of that term, that is, we do not worship a plurality of gods—multiple units in collection—and call that collection "god." We worship a living, moving, and dynamic God who engages humans in three distinct yet united "persons," namely, God the Father, God the Son, and God the Spirit. This threeness in oneness (and oneness in threeness) creates living movement within God's being, thereby allowing the Godhead to express itself uniformly yet distinctively. At any given time for some agreed-upon plan, the Trinity moves into action as Father, Son, and Spirit, in order to produce a desired result. There is perfect unity of will and action in the Trinity. We have no earthly counterpart to this divine reality that resembles our God as Triune: not the three-leaf clover, not the egg (shell, yolk, white), not even three forms of water (liquid, solid, gas). The Trinity is unique, and above our limited understanding. Therefore, our words to describe this God of Scripture falter at any adequacy to portray their object in fullness.

Yet it is this very Triune God who comes to us, reaching out as God the Son who enters human flesh, God the Father who sends the Son, and God the Spirit who is sent by Father and Son to the community of believers. Does this nature of God's being provide Christians with any sense of how we should live our human lives reflecting God's nature? I think it does. While humans are not God and cannot reflect the distinction and unity within the Trinity to any degree of precision, we are being transformed by this God into the image of Christ, who lives and reigns with the Father and the Spirit. Therefore, how we live in this world and live together in the church can be influenced by this Triune nature.

The Trinity lives in such continuous movement of unison that the early church called this *perichoresis* or a "choreographed dance" of the three persons of the Godhead. This word comes from two Greek words (*peri* + *choresis*), which mean to "move around" or "dance around." The Father, Son, and Spirit move so perfectly together in their functions—both toward each other and those outside of the Godhead—that if one were able to stand outside of the Trinity and view the movement of the Three in One/One in Three, it would be a blur resulting in unified action. Why? Because the movement of the Trinity to fulfill any one function that they have agreed upon is so uniform that when humans observe the revelation of God at work toward us, it is as if they are undivided.

The early church also had a Latin expression for this truth: *opera trinitatis ad extra indivisa sunt* ("the works of the Trinity toward that which is outside of it are undivided"). So, while God the Father may be seen as the Creator of the universe from various parts of Scripture, we also know that there is no creation without the Son (John 1:1; Hebrews 11:1–3) or the Spirit (Genesis 1:2). While God the Father may be called the "point person" of the work of creation—that is, the person of the Trinity who has leadership of and responsibility for this particular function—Christian theology asserts that God the Son and God the Spirit are also intimately involved. As the love that unites the Trinity together in their being and function, the Holy Spirit is also taking point, directing the movement of the Triune God outside of itself to the creation and redemption of the world. This is the one *missio Dei* of the Triune God.

The Mission of the Holy Spirit

Within the Triune God's overall plan, the Holy Spirit plays a specific role—one that is similar to the role played within the Trinitarian *perichoresis* itself; namely, the Spirit moves the Godhead toward others outside the divine life—toward those unlike God. Canadian theologian, Clark Pinnock, has described this role vividly by suggesting that the Spirit "completes the trinitarian circle and opens it up to the world outside God."[5] It is the role of the Spirit within the Trinitarian life to "trigger the overflow of God's pure benevolence" to what is "nondivine" or creaturely.[6] The richness of communion within the Triune God is so magnificent that the Spirit directs the overflow toward those outside of God. It is for this reason that Paul can say in Romans 5:5 that "God's love has been poured into our hearts through the Holy Spirit that has been given to us" (NRSV).

In a very real sense, it is right to see the Holy Spirit as a missionary who reaches out to the radically other in order to fulfill the *missio Dei*—or more accurately, the *missio trinitatis* (mission of the Trinity). By reaching out to those most unlike God, the Spirit demonstrates the church's own mission of reaching out to the radically other. Just as the Spirit triggers the overflow of the Triune God's love and life from within the inner-trinitarian fellowship to those outside of that fellowship, so too the Spirit triggers the overflow of God's love that has been poured into our human hearts so that we turn toward those most unlike us with a love that is both sincere and divine. The God of the people of God is a missionary and therefore the life of the church must reflect this heart of their God. As Daniel Migliore has noted, "A proper understanding of the church and its mission begins with this recognition: that the triune God initiates mission and the church is called to participate in that mission."[7]

What does the Spirit do as the "missionary God"? The Spirit points humans to Jesus Christ. There exists in the Holy Spirit a genuine humility—a preference to point people away from the Spirit and toward the Son of God. One might even describe this act as self-deferential. It pleases God the Father to place all things in heaven and earth under Christ's feet. Until that final day of consummation, it is the Spirit's task to draw humans to Christ. While possessing all the features and essence of divinity, the Spirit's

5. Pinnock, *Flame of Love*, 38.

6. Pinnock, *Flame of Love*, 38.

7. Migliore, "Missionary God," 18.

role is not to speak of himself, but to testify of the One who came in flesh to procure our salvation.[8] It is only as we point humans to Christ—not to ourselves!—that we can assure ourselves we are beginning to follow the *missio Dei* and, in particular, the *missio Spiritus* (mission of the Spirit).[9]

The Nature of the Church and the Spirit

Having considered the nature and mission of the Spirit as a foundation for the Spirit's indispensability in the church's mission, we are now ready to examine the nature and mission of the church, so as to underscore the necessity of the Spirit in the mission of the church. Who is the church and what are we called to do? As the people called out of darkness into light by her Lord, the church is formed by the power of the Spirit through regeneration of individuals and transformation of human lives. In some mysterious yet real way, the Spirit inserts believers into the Body of Christ, binding us together with Christ and each other by the Spirit's own presence. While Christ is the head of the church, the Holy Spirit is Lord over her mission.

The church, then, is a collection of regenerated people who have been delivered and transformed by Christ through the Spirit and have been engrafted into the spiritual body of Christ through that same Spirit. The church is the people of God who are called to assemble together in the name of Christ and are challenged to be Christ to the world. Only through the initiation of the Spirit's work in our lives—individually and corporately—can we hope to achieve the mission that our Master has given us.

Such a gracious movement of the Spirit in the life of the church does not mean that the church owns or possesses the Spirit so that the church can "control" the Spirit. As noted by the theologian Karl Barth, "There does not belong to [the church] the power of the sending and outpouring and operation of the Holy Spirit. [The church] does not 'possess' him. It cannot create or control him. He is promised to it. It can only receive Him and then be obedient to Him."[10] The church does not tell the Spirit where and when

8. Adam Dodds calls this the "anonymity" aspect of the Spirit's work, and one that he believes must be a part of the Church's mission as well. See Dodds, "Mission of the Spirit," 209–26.

9. A theological way to describe this idea is that pneumatology and Christology belong together. The mission of the Son and the mission of the Spirit intersect and overlap. It may be true that they are not entirely the same, but the differences do not need to be our focus here.

10. Barth, *Church Dogmatics*, 655.

it will move in mission; it does not determine to whom it will minister (or not!). It must remain solely the responsibility of the Spirit to initiate our mission when, where, and to whom the Spirit wills. It is our responsibility to listen and obey. Our mission is to move outward to the radically other, and only the Spirit can impel us outward in this way.

The Mission of the Church and the Spirit

In recent years, a theological movement with regard to the mission of the church has begun to spread throughout North America and many other parts of the world. It has been called the missional church movement. A central feature of this movement is that mission (or missions) is more than a "program" directed from the local church outward; mission is the centerpiece for the meaning of the church. Rather than making missions one more program in a series of churchly programs, this movement has asked the incisive question, "What is the heart of God with regard to our mission?" The resultant answer has been both shocking and stimulating to the church. Mission is not just a program within the church; it is the essence of our identity as the people of God who have been called and sent out. In the words of missional theologian Darrell Guder, mission "defines the church as God's sent people. Either we are defined by mission, or we reduce the scope of the gospel and the mandate of the church. Thus our challenge today is to move from church with mission to missional church."[11]

The missional movement has asked the church to reconsider its purpose and function in the world by realigning itself with the directional flow of God's own mission. What is the *missio Dei* (mission of God)? How can humans work within that mission as members of the body of Christ ministering to a needy world of humanity? I would suggest that a major contribution to the missional church movement is the development of a greater understanding of the role of the Spirit in helping us to jump into the river of God's own mission to the world. Without the Spirit, there is no missional goal—only human goals set by imperfect vessels.

The Holy Spirit provides the people of God with passion and purpose for its mission and ministry. What does this mean? Once the Spirit has brought us into God's kingdom, then the Spirit continues to work in us and alongside of us so that we might perform the good works that God has prepared in advance that we should do (Eph 2:10). For some reason, God

---

11. Guder, "Missional Church," 6.

has chosen to use weak, human vessels to share the good news. The Spirit works with us and in us in order to place the mission of God deeply within our psyche, and allows it to burn with passion, as it does in God's own heart. God has entrusted into human hands the message of reconciliation (2 Cor 5:18–21). What a privilege, and a responsibility! Given the enormity of this task, who would be so foolish to assume that we could accomplish it without the Spirit?

So then, precisely what is our mission to this world? In brief, it is to be Christ to our fellow humans. In many respects, the mission of the church today is really an extension of the mission of Christ—indeed, it is the ministry of Christ done through us by the power and direction of the Spirit. This is not a calling solely for people in full-time ministry, but for each person in the church who has been redeemed and transformed by the Spirit. It could be said that baptism into Jesus Christ is the ordination of every believer into ministry!

When the church turns to minister to the downtrodden in its neighborhood, it is never alone. The presence of the Risen Lord is with us through the mediating power of the Spirit. In a very real sense, our actions in ministry may appear entirely human, but the Spirit of God is working through our human hands in ways quite similar to the Spirit's working through the hands of Christ. Now our hands become—through the power of the Spirit—the hands of Christ, extended to humans in need. The Spirit is able to take our feeble attempts to obey and infuse them with a divine power, so that our words and efforts become tools that sink deeply to the core of those to whom we are ministering. The end result is that God the Spirit has worked in us and through us for the benefit of the individuals with whom we are sharing our lives. It is Christ in us who ministers life. Only when this occurs—when our frail attempts become the Spirit's instruments—does true and effective ministry occur on a level that no human being could have calculated or understood. This is part of the *missio Spiritus*. The great need in the church today is for believers to become "little Christs" in the world. The great tragedy in the church today is that believers and churches have come to the world in their own human strength, and not in the power of the Spirit who points people to Christ.

What should this ministry look like? Ray Anderson has suggested a poignant model based on the Greek word used to describe the Holy Spirit as "comforter" or "advocate." It is the word *paraklesis*. It contains the idea of someone being called alongside of another for the purpose of helping. We continue the ministry of Christ through the empowering ministry of *paraklesis* by the Spirit.[12] As Anderson describes this method of ministry, it is not located in teaching or preaching per se, but in presence—the presence of Christ through the Spirit in the lives of believers who are reaching out to others in their despair. Rather than solely verbal or intellectual, this ministry is relational. It is incarnational, it is Emmanuel; God is with us, even in our darkest ditch. Indeed, just as the Holy Spirit comes alongside us to help us in our hour of need, so God the Spirit ministers through believers to bring the presence of the Risen Christ to those in need.

Hence, the role of the Spirit in the church's ministry is one that continues the ministry of Christ here and now. Just as Jesus relied on the Spirit's anointing in order to preach good news to the poor, deliverance to captives, recovery of sight to the blind, and usher in the year of the Lord's favor, the church today must also rely on the Spirit for its direction (purpose) and its efficacy of ministry (power).

The Relational Spirit who Builds Community

Since the nature of our God is to live in community as Father, Son, and Spirit, it is also within the nature of humans—made in God's image—to live in communal relationality as well. However, sin has damaged our relationships and cast us into solitary isolation, even within our so-called communities. The Spirit saves us from alienation and solitariness in order to bring us into a loving community of fellow believers (i.e., the church). For years in North America, we have defined "church" as a building or institution. Further, we have defined "success" in the church by some fiendish designation related to numbers of people in our buildings. If trends continue as they are currently, these ideas will need to disappear in any effective church during the next decade. People are no longer interested in going to a building to hear a sermon or listen to music, no matter how interesting the speaker or how hip the music! People want relationships that recognize their value. If we are to reach others for Christ, we will need to recognize this God-given yearning for deep relationships in each human heart.

12. Anderson, *Shape of Practical Theology*, 198–99. The word *paraklesis* comes from John 14 and 16, where Jesus speaks of the Spirit as the Comforter, Helper, or Advocate, whom he will send. It is also used in 1 John 2:1–2 to speak of Jesus Christ himself as our "advocate [*paraklete*] with the Father."

In actuality, only the Spirit can lift humans up from the miry pit through the work of Christ and draw us into the life—dare I say, the dance—of God. Indeed, this is one of the distinctive functions of the Spirit: "to bring persons into relationship while maintaining their otherness, their particular and unique freedom."[13] The church is the gathered, regenerated people of God who are being transformed into the likeness of Christ by the Spirit's power. We are people who reflect the nature of the God we serve—albeit imperfectly at times—because we have been encountered by this grace-filled God and are being transformed day-by-day with increasing glory (2 Cor 3:18). The purpose of the church is not to run programs to see how many people we can get into our places of worship, nor to circulate with people who look like us and act like us, and therefore people with whom we are comfortable socially. The purpose of the church is to demonstrate the character of Christ in all our actions, words, and reflections. It is to build community where relationships dive below the surface-level masks that we present to others. It is to engage here and now, in some sense, in the divine fellowship and wholeness that we will one day inhabit for eternity. Church should be a place where the gathered people of God reflect the nature of their God, and therefore live in a communion marked by eternity.

The Spirit sends us out of ourselves to seek and save the lost. The church, then, is this arm of God for sharing the good news (evangelism). Yet that is not the final task! In God's plan, there is a goal of relationship— one focused on God first and then neighbors second (Matt 22:37–40). Indeed, the entire theme of salvation in theology begins with deliverance and conversion, but that is not the end of it all. God has made humans for relationship with him. God wants to spend eternity with us, and therefore initiates and executes an eternal plan to redeem us back to his own life, thereby bringing us into union with the Triune God.[14]

If God's plan is focused on relationships, then it is the Spirit who is charged with bringing unity and the "bond of peace" to the Body of Christ (Eph 4:3). Yet anyone who has worked with church people knows that this ideal is rarely achieved among church-attenders. Indeed, the more complete rendering of that verse from Paul stresses that humans must do something as well: "Make every effort to keep the unity of the Spirit through the bond of peace" (Eph 4:3). Building relationships with people who are unlike us

13. Gunton, *Promise of Trinitarian Theology*, 136.

14. Clark Pinnock describes this feature of salvation insightfully in *Flame of Love*, 149–84.

is risky business! Indeed, it is clear from the New Testament that we have tragic examples of where such efforts can land when our fleshly desires lead us instead of the Spirit. Consider the example of cliques at Corinth. Yet the Spirit continues to work with us in order to help us reflect the character of our God. It is the Spirit's task to make us look like Christ—to live like our master within the current contexts of the twenty-first century. When the world looks at the church, too often it sees division within it. Lesslie Newbigin has called such division a "violent contradiction of [the church's] own fundamental nature."[15] If we are reconciled with God through the work of Christ and the application of the Spirit to our lives, then how can we remain divided from other members of the body of Christ? What witness does this give concerning the truth and reality of the ministry of reconciliation? Why should we even try to restore and reconcile relationships inside the church when it seems that we can never achieve a perfect harmony here and now?

The reason that we must work toward reconciliation within the body of Christ is precisely because the Holy Spirit is working this reality within us here and now. We must add to God's gracious work in us the responsive effort of our own lives, so that the end result will be a truer reflection of the God who comes to reconcile the whole world. The Holy Spirit works the holy character of Christ into our lives so that we, too, become focused and centered on the other—those unlike us socially, politically, economically, yet like us in the fact that we all have sinned and come short of the glory of God (Rom 3:23). We must obey and "make every effort" to build on this unity of the Spirit. The Spirit weaves God's people together into a spiritual bond between God and them—helping us overcome our apparent differences so that we might build holy and effective relationships within the context of submitted discipleship. Without the Spirit, there is no relational church—only a social gathering of look-alikes!

Conclusion

In light of what has been considered thus far, what is the church to do? Allow me to suggest four practical responses:

The church must first learn to be in relationship with the Triune God before it tries to do something. In its best form, ministry is birthed out of resting in the presence and life of God where one receives energy, life, and

---

15. Newbigin, *Household of God*, 18.

direction for action. Hence, prayer as relation-building and meditative focus on God is an essential component for ministry and corporate mission.

The church must listen to the Spirit, the Lord of her missional task. Without the direction of the Spirit, we will launch into well-intentioned programs that may achieve some "success," but will not endure for eternity.

Third, the church must align herself with the *missio Dei* in this world. Navigating the cultural hoops and expectations of the church in the twenty-first century makes it exponentially more difficult to recognize the heart of God's mission. We must look to the Scriptures and to our own prayer lives in order to discern the direction of God's heart for this world today.

Finally, the church must be Christ extended to the world. Humans may help other humans, but humans cannot save humans. Only God can do this! Therefore, the church directs attention to the Savior of the world, not to some feeble human replacement. People need to see Jesus Christ, not us. It is the Spirit's task to conform us to the image of Christ; it is our task to let him do this, so that when others observe the people of God, they will see the face of God the Father through the image of God the Son.[16] Only God the Spirit can bring about such a transformation in us. Only a church transformed into the image of Christ will provide authentic witness to the reality of our God in front of a skeptical, religion-weary (and religion-wary) world. Come, Holy Spirit!

Questions for Reflection

1. Theologians have attempted to simplify the understanding of the Trinity by providing analogies to things on Earth: the three-leaf clover, the egg (shell, yoke, white), or three forms of water (liquid, solid, gas). Why are these analogies not helpful if one is growing deeper in their understanding of the Triune God?

2. When you think about how Father, Son, and Spirit are one and yet three in their inner life, how does the idea of movement or dance assist you in that reflection?

---

16. Torrance, *Theology in Reconstruction*, 252. Thomas Torrance has used a similar phrase concerning the Spirit. I have borrowed it here for my purposes. Torrance says of the Spirit, "He does not show his own face, but shows us the Father in the face of the Son."

3. Reflect on the significance of viewing the Spirit as the trigger for the overflow of divine love. What does this mean for the Trinity and for the church?

4. "It must remain solely the responsibility of the Spirit to initiate our mission when, where, and to whom the Spirit wills. It is our responsibility to listen and obey." What does this listening and obeying look like in the local church? (In other words, how do we listen and obey the Spirit?)

5. The mission of the church today is really an extension of the mission of Christ, in the power of the Spirit. What are some specific ways that you can see the work of the church as an extension of the mission of Christ?

6. If churches today focused more on Christ's mission and on the *paracletic* ministry of the Spirit, what would be different and what would be the same?

For Further Reading

Bolsinger, Tod E. *It Takes a Church to Raise a Christian: How the Community of God Transforms Lives*. Grand Rapids: Brazos, 2004.

Green, Chris E. W., ed. *Pentecostal Ecclesiology: A Reader*. Leiden, Netherlands: Brill, 2016.

Marshall, Molly Truman. *Joining the Dance: A Theology of the Spirit*. King of Prussia, PA: Judson, 2003.

Moltmann, Jürgen. *The Church in the Power of the Spirit: A Contribution to Messianic Ecclesiology*. Translated by Margaret Kohl. Minneapolis: Fortress, 1993.

Pinnock, Clark. *Flame of Love: A Theology of the Holy Spirit*. Downers Grove: InterVarsity, 1996.

The Power of Prayer

Henry J. Smith, DMin[1]

Therefore confess your sins to each other and pray
for each other so that you may be healed.
The prayer of a righteous man is powerful
and effective.

—Jas 5:16[2]

IT IS A GIVEN that all believers will pray, but all believers do not pray in the same way. Some may pray aloud, while others may pray in silence. Some may kneel, others may stand or sit, yet all are communicating with God. Prayer should always be a true communication with God, and not done for public recognition.

How can we define prayer? Prayer is communication with God. It is the expression of our inner spiritual needs. It is a dialogue with God, speaking to him and listening for a response from him. Prayer is an expression of our faith and trust in God. It is an expression of our thankfulness for who God is and what he has done for us. In a general sense, prayer is the act of asking for a favor. The Scriptures tell us that prayer is giving adoration

1. Henry Smith serves as a Senior Adjunct Professor in the Christian Ministries Department at Lee University. Dr. Smith is a graduate of California Graduate School of Theology, with a DMin degree in Religious Studies. His background includes fifteen years as pastor of local church congregations, and more than forty years as administrator and classroom instructor in religious institutions. He is the author of a book of prophecy, *The Time of the End*. He has also written many articles for church publications.

2. All Scripture quotations are from the New International Version (NIV) unless otherwise noted.

to God, confessing our sins, asking for mercy and forgiveness. It is also a means of expressing our dedication to God's service and interceding for the needs of others It is not a "quick fix" for our problems. God answers prayer in his own way and in his own time (Ps 40:1–3).

Prayer is the golden key which unlocks the treasury of God and brings blessings to his children. The Scriptures enjoin upon us the practice of prayer. Prayer consists of communion, petition, and intercession. The first two serve to store the heart with the grace of God, while the latter extends it to the welfare of others.

You may have heard the statement "Prayer changes things." It refers to the power of prayer. I had the privilege of being raised in a family that believed in the power of prayer. Posted on the wall of our family room were these words "Prayer changes things." We lived by this statement—we believed that God possesses the power to do any and all things. On one occasion, my mother prayed that her baby, my sister, would be healed from seizures; she was having as many as ten seizures a day. After my mother prayed, my sister had no more seizures. On another occasion, my father, who was a minister, prayed for a six-year-old playmate of mine who was blind in his left eye. After prayer, the young boy had perfect vision in his left eye. As an adult, I can give witness to God's power, having experienced many outstanding works of God.

Prayer in the Old Testament

Many Old Testament saints understood the power of prayer: "At that time men began to call on the name of the Lord" (Gen 4:26). This seems to be the beginning of prayer. From this point forward, we read of many men and women who used the means of prayer to communicate with God. Abraham was a man of prayer. Through his dedication, God gave him and Sarah a son, even in their old age (Gen 21). He prayed for Lot, and Lot was delivered from destruction, (Gen 19). Moses prayed and God opened the Red Sea, and allowed the children of Israel to cross on dry land (Exod 14). Elijah prayed and no rain fell for three-and-a-half years (1 Kgs 17). He prayed again and God sent fire to consume wet wood, thereby proving to Israel that he was the true God (1 Kgs 18). Elisha prayed and the Shunammite's son was brought back to life (2 Kgs 4). Daniel prayed and he was delivered from the lion's den (Dan 6). King Hezekiah prayed and his life was extended (2 Kgs 20). Hannah prayed and God gave her a son, who became a great judge in Israel (1 Sam 1) In addition to Hannah, there are other Old Testament women who, without a doubt, were women of faith and prayer.

Even though Sarah doubted the promise of God that she would have a child in her old age, she came to understand that he was faithful. She is listed in Hebrews chapter 11 as one of the heroes of faith. Rahab is also listed as a hero of the faith in the same chapter. The Scripture does not record her prayer; yet we know that she communicated with God and was greatly honored by him. Then there is Esther who, along with her maids, fasted in order to receive God's guidance and blessings. We are not told that she prayed; yet we are taught in Scripture that prayer and fasting go hand in hand. By seeking God, Esther was able to save her people from destruction.

The writer of the book of Hebrews tells us of many others who experience many blessings because of their faith in God and the prayers they prayed to him (again, see Hebrews 11).

Jesus and Prayer

Jesus understood the power of prayer. He spent many hours in prayer. Often he went to a solitary place and prayed for hours at a time (Matt 14:23; Mark 1:35; Luke 5:16). Jesus prayed for many things and for many people. He prayed for little children (Matt 19:13) and for his disciples (John 17). Jesus taught us the value of private prayer "But when you pray, go into your room, close the door and pray to your Father, who is unseen. Then your Father, who sees what is done in secret, will reward you" (Matt 6:6). Jesus also gave approval of public prayer.

Mark tells us that Jesus prayed and five loaves and two fish were multiplied, so that five thousand men were able to eat until they were filled (Mark 6:39–44). One of the great prayers of Jesus was at the tomb of Lazarus: "Then Jesus looked up and said, 'Father I thank you that you have heard me. I knew that you always hear me, but I said this for the benefit of the people standing here, that they may believe that you sent me.' When he had said this, Jesus called in a loud voice, 'Lazarus, come out'" (John 11:41–43).

As Jesus was approaching his final days on Earth in human form, he went to the Mount of Olives for a time of prayer: "He withdrew about a stone's throw beyond them, knelt down and prayed. 'Father, if you are willing, take this cup from me; yet not my will, but yours be done'" (Luke 22:41–42).

In John chapter 17, Jesus prayed three prayers. First, he prayed for himself: "Father, the hour has come, Glorify your Son, that your Son may glorify you . . . I have brought you glory on earth by finishing the work you gave me to do. And now, Father, glorify me in your presence with the glory I had with you before the world began" (John 17:1–5). Next, he prayed for his disciples: "I pray for them. I am not praying for the world, but for those you have given me, for they are yours" (John 17:9). Finally, he prayed for all believers. "My prayer is not for them alone. I pray also for those who will believe in me through their message, that all of them may be one . . . Father, I want those you have given me to be with me where I am, and to see my glory, the glory you have given me because you loved me before the creation of the world" (John 17:20–21, 24).

At the request of his disciples, Jesus taught them how to pray:

> This, then, is how you should pray: "Our Father in heaven, hallowed be your name. Your kingdom come, your will be done, on earth as it is in heaven. Give us today our daily bread. And forgive us our debts, as we also have forgiven our debtors. And lead us not into temptation, but deliver us from the evil one." For if you forgive other people when they sin against you, your heavenly Father will also forgive you. But if you do not forgive others their sins, your Father will not forgive your sins. (Matt 6:9–15)

This is most often referred to as the Lord's Prayer. It was, in fact, the disciple's prayer, and it is a prayer for all believers today. As a believer, we often recite this prayer, and that it good; however, it is more important to live by the principles laid out in the prayer.

Jesus teaches believers to be direct and specific when they approach God in prayer: "And when you pray, do not keep on babbling like pagans, for they think they will be heard because of their many words. Do not be like them, for your Father knows what you need before you ask him" (Matt 6:7–8). It is not the number of words we say, or how eloquently we say them, that counts with God. It is the sincerity of our words that matters to him. We must remember that prayer is not a monologue, but a dialogue. It is essential that God's voice responds to ours, or our prayers will be without effect. Let us understand that God always responds when our prayer is in the right spirit and in harmony with his will.

Our Lord made many other statements about prayer: "Ask and it will be given to you; seek and you will find; knock and the door will be opened to you. For everyone who asks receives; the one who seeks finds; and to the one who knocks, the door will be opened" (Matt 7:7–8); "If you believe, you will receive whatever you ask for in prayer" (Matt 21:22); "And I will do whatever you ask in my name, so that the Father may be glorified in the Son. You may ask me for anything in my name, and I will do it" (John 14:13–14); "Therefore I tell you, whatever you ask for in prayer, believe that you have received it, and it will be yours" (Mark 11:24). We must pray that his will, not ours, be done. We must pray in faith, knowing that our Lord is concerned about our every need.

In the parable of the pharisee and the tax collector, Jesus gives us an example of the right way and the wrong way to pray:

> Two men went up to the temple to pray, one a Pharisee and the other a tax collector. The Pharisee stood by himself and prayed: "God, I thank you that I am not like other people—robbers, evil-doers, adulterers—or even like this tax collector. I fast twice a week and give a tenth of all I get." But the tax collector stood at a distance. He would not even look up to heaven, but beat his breast and said, "God have mercy on me, a sinner." I tell you that this man, rather than the other, went home justified before God. For all those who exalt themselves will be humbled, and those who humble themselves will be exalted. (Luke 18:10–14)

May God help us all to learn from this parable.

Prayer in the New Testament

After the ascension of Jesus, the disciples depended upon prayer as a means of communicating with the Godhead. Upon returning to Jerusalem, "They all joined together constantly in prayer, along with the women and Mary the mother of Jesus, and with his brothers" (Acts 1:14). One of the first prayers that the apostles prayed was that God would give his choice for a replacement for Judas: "'Lord, you know everyone's heart. Show us which of these two you have chosen to take over this apostolic ministry, which Judas left to go where he belongs.' Then they cast lots, and the lot fell to Matthias; so he was added to the eleven apostles" (Acts 1:24–26). After the great Pentecostal experience, being filled with the Holy Spirit, they spent much time in prayer: "They devoted themselves to the apostles' teaching and to the fellowship, to the breaking of bread and to prayer" (Acts 2:42).

Stephen, one of the seven selected to take care of the needs of the widows of the early church, began to be used by God to preach the good news of the risen Christ. Soon he was brought before the Jewish rulers and was put to death. As he was being stoned, "he fell on his knees and cried out, 'Lord, do not hold this sin against them.' When he had said this, he fell asleep" (Acts 7:60). His prayer was very much like the one Jesus prayed from the cross.

When Peter was put in prison for preaching the gospel, the believers went to their knees in prayer: "So Peter was kept in prison, but the church was earnestly praying to God for him" (Acts 12:5). God responded to their prayers and sent an angel to deliver Peter from prison. When Peter arrived at the house where they were praying, they did not believe that it was him. The power of prayer was so great that it was beyond their understanding.

When Paul and Silas were imprisoned at Philippi, they turned to prayer: "About midnight Paul and Silas were praying and singing hymns to God, and the other prisoners were listening to them. Suddenly there was such a violent earthquake that the foundations of the prison were shaken. At once all the prison doors flew open, and everyone's chains came loose" (Acts 16:25–26). As the result of their faithfulness and prayers, they were set free, and the keeper of the prison and his family became followers of Christ.

Paul understood the necessity of prayer and the power thereof. "And pray in the Spirit on all occasions with all kinds of prayers and requests . . . and always keep on praying for all the Lord's people. Pray also for me" (Eph 6:18–19). Paul recorded many Spirit-inspired prayers throughout his thirteen books of the New Testament. Praying and learning his prayers can help us deepen and strengthen our prayer lives. It is my prayer that God will use the prayers of Paul to transform the life of my readers. Let us take a look at some of the prayers of Paul: "Brothers, my heart's desire and prayer to God for the Israelites is that they may be saved" (Rom 10:1); "Be joyful in hope, patient in affliction, faithful in prayer" (Rom 12:12); "May the God of hope fill you with all joy and peace as you trust in him, so that you may overflow with hope by the power of the Holy Spirit" (Rom 15:13).

Not only did Paul pray for others, he asked others to pray for him:

> I urge you, brothers and sisters, by our Lord Jesus Christ and by the love of the Spirit, to join me in my struggle by praying to God for me. Pray that I may be kept safe from the unbelievers in Judea and that the contribution I take to Jerusalem may be favorably received by the Lord's people, so that I may come to you with joy, by God's will, and in your company be refreshed. The God of peace be with you all. Amen. (Rom 15:30–33)

Paul was asking other believers to become intercessors on his behalf. May we learn how to become intercessors for those in a time of need.

On many occasions, Paul prayed prayers of thanksgiving. He was expressing thanks to God and to fellow believers. Great examples of this kind of prayers are found in Paul's letters to the believers in Corinth: "I always thank God for you because of his grace given you in Christ Jesus. For in him you have been enriched in every way" (1 Cor 1:4–5); "Praise be to the God and Father of our Lord Jesus Christ, the Father of compassion and the God of all comfort, who comforts us in all our troubles, so that we can comfort those in any trouble with the comfort we ourselves have received from God" (2 Cor 1:3–4); "But thanks be to God, who always leads us as captives in Christ's triumphal procession and uses us to spread the aroma of the knowledge of him everywhere. For we are to God the pleasing aroma of Christ among those who are being saved" (2 Cor 2:14–15).

Paul not only prayed for believers in Corinth; he also prayed for the Ephesians, the Philippians, the Colossians, and many others: "Praise be to the God and Father of our Lord Jesus Christ, who has blessed us in the heavenly realms with every spiritual blessing in Christ" (Eph 1:3); "For this reason, ever since I heard about your faith in the Lord Jesus and your love for all God's people, I have not stopped giving thanks for you, remembering you in my prayers" (Eph 1:15–16); "I thank my God every time I remember you. In all my prayers for all of you, I always pray with joy because of you partnership in the gospel" (Phil 1:3–5); "We always thank God for all of you and continually mention you in our prayers. We remember before our God and Father your work produced by faith, your labor prompted by love, and your endurance inspired by hope in our Lord Jesus Christ" (1 Thess 1:2–3).

The prayer that Paul prayed for Philemon is no doubt a prayer that he would pray for all believers. It is a prayer that believers today can and should pray for each other: "I always thank my God as I remember you in my prayers, because I hear about your love for all his holy people and your faith in the Lord Jesus. I pray that your partnership with us in the faith may be effective in deepening your understanding of every good thing we share for the sake of Christ. Your love has given me great joy and encouragement, because you, brother, have refreshed the hearts of the Lord's people" (Phlm 4–7).

Women of prayer were a large part of the first-century body of Christ. Mary the mother of Jesus, when told that she would have a son even though she was a virgin, said, "I am the Lord's servant . . . May your word to be me fulfilled" (Luke 1:38). Women were involved in prayer prior to the Day of Pentecost, while the believers were waiting for the promise from God: "They all joined together constantly in prayer, along with the women and Mary the mother of Jesus" (Acts 1:14). When Peter was in prison, men and women believers gathered together and prayed for his release. They met in the home of Mary, the mother of John Mark. God responded to their prayers and set Peter free (Acts 12:12).

The writer of Hebrews encourages believers to approach God in prayer: "Let us then approach God's throne of grace with confidence, so that we may receive mercy and find grace to help is in in our time of need" (Heb 4:16). James was a strong believer in the value of prayer: "If any of you lacks wisdom, you should ask God, who gives generously to all without finding fault, and it will be given to you" (Jas 1:5). Writing to the Corinthians, Paul points out that women in their congregation were not only praying, but also prophesying (1 Cor 11:3–16). How then can we doubt the value of prayer? New Testament writers firmly believed that God would hear them when they prayed, and that he would respond according to his will.

How Then Should We Pray?

We can see from Biblical examples, as well as the words of Jesus, that believers are to connect with God in prayer. The word tells us to "Pray without ceasing" (1 Thess 5:17). The Bible lets us know that there is power in prayer. Great men of God, such as John Knox, John Wesley, Charles Finney, and D. L. Moody, were all men of prayer. They all attribute the success of their ministry to prayer.

As believers, we should approach God as our loving heavenly Father. As we approach him, we should understand that he desires to do good things for us: "how much more will your Father in heaven give good gifts to those who ask him" (Matt 7:11). We should approach him with an attitude of gratitude—thanking him for who he is and for what he has done for us, for forgiving our sins, for supplying our needs, and for giving us the gift of eternal life.

When we pray, we should pray in faith, believing that God hears our prayer and will answer in his own time and in his own way: "This is the confidence we have in approaching God: that if we ask anything according to his will, he hears us. And if we know that he hears us—whatever we ask—we know that we have what we asked of him" (1 John 5:14–15).

The writer of Hebrews reminds us that, without faith, it is impossible to please God. The prophet Isaiah also reminds us that our prayers are heard by God: "Before they call I will answer; while they are still speaking I will hear" (Isa 65:24).

Jesus said that we are to ask for the things we desire from God. We are to ask, even though Jesus also said, "your Father knows what you need before you ask him" (Matt 6:8). Often we must be persistent in prayer, as was the man in Luke 11:5–8. Sometimes, the answer to our prayers may be different than what we expected. Paul prayed three times that a thorn in his flesh would be removed, but God said no, my grace is sufficient for you. We must remember that God is never late; he is always on time, not out time, but his.

Conclusion

When Jesus taught his disciples to pray, he did not say "if" you pray, but "when." These words teach us that all believers are to pray. Our prayers should include adoration, thanksgiving, petition, confession, praise, and intercession. Prayer is vital part of the mission of the church. A praying church is a loving, helping, and soul-winning family of God. A praying church is one that is making disciples and sharing the gospel with a lost world. We must remember that prayer and service go together. Prayer without service is only a dream. Service without prayer amounts to little. We are to pray with a thankful heart and with faith. We must continue in prayer; that is, maintaining a consistent prayer life.

Prayer is a mighty weapon, a weapon that can be used to defeat the evil one. We know from Scripture that prayer preserved Job, converted Paul, restored Peter, and shook Jerusalem with a mighty revival. Prayer closed the mouths of lions, quenched the violence of fire, broke down prison bars, cast out devils, and raised the dead.

John Wesley, the father of Methodism, recognized the power of prayer when he said: "Give me 100 preachers who fear nothing but sin and desire nothing but God, and I care not a straw whether they be clergy or laymen, such alone will shake the gates of hell and set up the kingdom of Heaven on earth. God does nothing but in answer to prayer."[3] C. H. Spurgeon, the English Baptist preacher of the nineteenth century, knew the power of prayer. On one occasion, he said, "Through prayer, God greatly multiplies our ef-

---

3. Maxwell, *Partners in Prayer*, 7.

forts. Whenever God determines to do a great work, he first sets His people to pray."[4] Billy Graham understood the power of prayer. Reflecting upon the great Los Angeles crusade, he said: "The only difference between the L. A. crusade and all the others before it had been the amount of prayer her and his people had given it."[5] As believers may, we follow in the footsteps of our praying fathers of the faith, for indeed there is power in prayer.

Questions for Reflection

1. As you reflect upon the concepts of prayer, what is your understanding of the need of prayer in the life of a believer?

2. How is prayer in Old Testament times different from prayer in New Testament times? Or is prayer the same in both periods?

3. Since Jesus was the Son of God, why did he feel the need to spend many hours in prayer?

4. Give some thought to the prayer that Jesus taught us to pray. Are you following the principles set forth in prayer?

For Further Reading

Bradshaw, Timothy. *Praying as Believing: The Lord's Prayer and the Christian Doctrine of God*. Macon, GA: Smyth & Helwys, 1998.

Maxwell, John. *Partners in Prayer*. Nashville: Thomas Nelson, 1996.

LaHaye, Beverly. *Prayer: God's Comfort for Today's Family*. Nashville: Thomas Nelson, 1990.

Lockyer, Herbert. *All the Prayers of the Bible*. Grand Rapids: Zondervan, 1959.

London, H. B., Jr., and Neil B. Wiseman. *The Heart of a Great Pastor*. Ventura, CA: Regal, 1994.

Small, P. Douglas. *Prayer: The Heart of It All: Biblical Principles with Practical Models*. Kannapolis, NC: Alive, 2017.

4. Maxwell, *Partners in Prayer*, 7.

5. Maxwell, *Partners in Prayer*, 6.

The Necessity of Calling

Jimmy Harper, DMin[1]

For we are God's workmanship, created in Christ Jesus to do
good works which God has prepared in advance for us to do.

—Eph 2:10[2]

THERE IS A POPULAR worship song by Bethel Music entitled, "Have It All."
In that song, there is one lyric that reads, "There is no greater call, than
giving You my all." The lyrics sound great, but those words are difficult to
live out in daily life. There seems to be a deep-seated desire in most people
to live a life of impact. Giving oneself to be used by God is certainly one
way to bring impact. However, how is that goal accomplished? How can
individuals genuinely follow their call by giving God their all?

For decades, Americans have generally felt their career to be very important.[3] Many people describe the idea of career as the most important
aspect of a great life. However, there are other extremely significant factors.
About 75 percent of US adults seek out ways to live a more meaningful life,

---

1. Jimmy Harper serves as Campus Pastor and Assistant Professor of Youth & Family
Ministry at Lee University. Dr. Harper is a graduate of Fuller Seminary in Pasadena,
California, with a DMin in Church Ministry Studies. Jimmy ministered in local churches
for over fifteen years. He has nearly twenty years of experience in administration and
teaching at Lee University, has authored a book for youth ministry—*Launching A Forever Faith*—and has published many articles for local church ministry and national
publications.

2. All Scripture quotations are from the New International Version (NIV) unless
otherwise noted.

3. Barna, *What Americans Believe*, 149.

not only in their career, but also in their family, at church, or by engaging in other worthwhile projects. Additionally, almost 60 percent of adults say they desire to make a difference in their world. Adults seem to covet a commitment with a quality vocation. In other words, they feel "called" to make appropriate and quality decisions toward "certain types of work and life choices."[4] But is the idea of vocation one of work, or one of calling? There is a marked difference in the attitude toward these approaches.

What Is Calling?

The idea of "work" is often viewed as "employment; job; the means by which one earns one's livelihood."[5] "Calling," on the other hand, seems to emphasize "a summoning or inviting" of person by God to a special purpose within the body of Christ.[6] The call of God then, must play a major role as to how one determines one's vocation in life. The call of God will help individuals figure out what direction is the appropriate vocation. But in so doing, people must take care in allowing God to give proper guidance to the choices made along the way.

So practically, how is the idea of a calling lived out in view of God's work in the lives of believers? Watchman Nee was a persecuted church leader who understood the necessity and difficulty of living out one's call. Writing to other persecuted church leaders and members, he described the call of God in this very detailed and specific way:

> The calling of God is a distinctive calling. Moreover, its object is always precise; never merely haphazard or undefined. By this I mean that, when God commits to you or me a ministry, He does so not merely to occupy us in His service, but always to accomplish through each of us something definite towards the attaining of His goal. It is of course true that there is a general commission to His Church to "make disciples of all nations"; but to any one of us God's charge represents, and must always represent, a personal trust. He calls us to serve Him in the sphere of His choice, whether to confront His people with some special aspect of the fullness of Christ, or in some other particular relation to the divine plan.

4. Barna Group, "Three Trends," para. 1.

5. *American Heritage Dictionary*, 1390.

6. Packer, "Calling," 108.

To some degree at least, every ministry should be in that sense a specific ministry.[7]

Certainly, there is a general call for all believers to be involved in the kingdom of God through ministry. In the Old Testament, the call of God is best represented in the covenant he set up with the nation of Israel. Any individual call in the Old Testament is only understood in relation to the corporate destiny of Israel. In that way, God's calling represents a fulfillment of his purposes by his servants.[8]

In New Testament terms, the initial aspect of the call of God (*kaleo*) relates to our ability to have a relationship with him. The primary meaning of the word denotes an invitation or a summons to salvation in Christ, and ministry and service to his kingdom. This call goes out to everyone. We know from 2 Peter 3:9 that "The Lord is . . . not willing that any should perish, but that all should come to repentance." Of those who are called (*kletoi*), only those who respond to the call are chosen (*ekletoi*) (Matt 22:14).[9] A part of being in relationship with God means that we begin to interact and learn from him. This interaction should lead us to a life filled with total dependence on our Savior. Then and only then will we begin to understand what God desires for our life.

Those who respond to the call constitute the church. The New Testament church is, essentially, a living organism, needing all its parts to work together to function appropriately. First Corinthians 12:12–27 helps us to understand the working of the body of Christ by comparing it to the human body.[10] As the human body functions properly, its many parts work together in harmony and as a whole. In the same way, the body of Christ must have each member involved and working together if the church is to become what Christ would have it to be. The call of God is to live out the purpose of God in our daily life and in the life of the church.

There seems to be a secondary application to the meaning of "call" in the New Testament. God has given some within the body of Christ a specific call to be leaders within his body. New Testament terminology often uses the call of God in designating individuals for specific functions in the church within God's redemptive plan.[11] Again, in 1 Corinthians 12:28, the

7. Nee, *What Shall This Man Do?*, 9.

8. Davies, *Westminster Dictionary*, 73.

9. Packer, "Calling," 108.

10. Ogden, *Unfinished Business*, 19.

11. Packer, "Calling," 108.

word says that God gave leadership gifts to "some" of his body. Likewise, Ephesians 4:11–12 tells us that God gave certain leadership gifts to some members of the body so that those members could work with other members to bring them to maturity in their relationship with Christ.

In order for believers to know the path that God desires for them to take, there must be a deliberate investigation. People must look into the life events that have formed them into the people they are today. In other words, it is very important for every individual to pay attention to his or her personal story. Believers must be able to appreciate their experiences and then be able to perceive how those experiences guide them toward their calling for life. We must seek to understand the primary function we should fill. Then, there must be a focus on realizing God's plans in the life of the believer for the future.[12] Once the plan of God has been realized in our life, we can help others understand God's plan for their lives. Again, the beauty here is that our individual calling does not simply impact us, as an individual. Our calling has significant influence on the corporate Body of Christ. So, we are called by God individually, but our calling is lived out as we serve and minister in our community of faith.

Personal Calling

One of the most important features of understanding the personal call of God to you, as an individual, is to find the foundation of that call in the past. Experiences in life form a foundation upon which the call of God is realized in one's life. For that reason, if we overlook the past, we might overlook the starting point for knowing God's will for our ministry. If we miss this foundation for ministry, we may never come to a true understanding of what area of ministry will be the most beneficial for us and the body of Christ.

In the Old Testament, the most frequent command given to the people of Israel by God is to "remember." God has a way of helping his people stay connected to him as they remember what he has done for them throughout their history. In reality, God is trying to show his children that, no matter where they go in the future, they must be tied to him through their history with him.[13]

---

12. Walling, "Power Of A Focused Life," 2.
13. Walling, "Power Of A Focused Life," 4.

There are countless stories of the call of God in the lives of his people that help us to understand the connection our call has to our situations and circumstances in life. People who were hurt as kids have gone into a life of counseling others to help them recover from the pain of the past. People who have never heard the name of Jesus are saved and begin to live life as an evangelist, carrying the gospel that has changed their life. People who were rescued from a life of drugs, encouraged by a youth pastor who reached out to them, begin to reach others as a youth pastor. Our experiences have a way of launching us into a life of ministry.[14]

In reality, each individual is a product of life experiences. We take all of life's circumstances and utilize every one of them to form who we are. Usually, whether good or bad, the experiences affect us for the rest of our lives. Taking the past, then, and learning and growing from it, will help us move into the future with confidence. If we allow past experiences to be a teacher, we can move forward with high expectations of what God can and will do in our lives. When God leads, good things happen.

To Be or To Do?

Essential to understanding the leading of God is the necessity of differentiating between being and doing.[15] God has called all mankind to be in a relationship with him. In fact, 2 Peter 3:9 says, "The Lord is not slow in keeping his promise, as some understand slowness. Instead He is patient with you." As we enter into a relationship with God, we are to become his disciple—learn who he is and emulate his commitments to life. We have to learn to be like Jesus as we seek to follow him.[16]

Jesus called the disciples to follow him in the New Testament. As he called his disciples, "He ordained twelve, that they should be with Him, and that He might send them forth to preach" (Mark 3:14). Those whom Jesus would depend upon to carry the gospel to ends of the Earth needed to spend time with and learn from him. How can we be any different than his disciples today? The most important aspect of growing in him is to "be" with him and learn his ways. We can be with him in prayer. We can be with

14. These stories are anecdotal examples of calling, and are not tied to any particular individual or situation.

15. Cross, *Answering The Call*, 4.

16. For a discussion of what it means to follow Jesus in service and ministry, see Blanchard and Hodges, *Lead Like Jesus*.

him in reading his word. We can be with him spending time doing his work. We can be with him through fellowship with others who follow him. There are many ways we can be with God. But we must be with him to learn from him. Then, our learning helps us to be like God, and it helps us to hear his voice as he calls out to us to participate in ministry.

Abraham was called to go to a land which God would show him. If he would follow God, all the families of the Earth would be blessed (Gen 12). Moses was called by God, who appeared in the form of a burning bush, to deliver the Israelites out of the bondage of Egypt (Exod 3). God called Samuel to speak against the evil household of Eli (1 Sam 3). God called many throughout the Bible and throughout history with an audible voice and with a small whisper. Although God may call his children in various ways, he desires for each member of humanity to work for his kingdom. He wants all humankind to be engaged in a relationship with him and to be used in this world for good works (Eph 2:10).

If we are able to spend quality time getting to know Jesus, if we can learn to model our lives after him, and if we can follow him consistently as we live out our daily existence, we will gain an understanding as to who we really are in Jesus. We will know what it means to be redeemed, delivered, justified, regenerated, and made alive in Christ. We can understand the richness of his grace, love, mercy, and blessings in our lives. We can identify the kind of relationship that helps us live for him and allows him to live in and through us. We will be in a committed relationship that will help us to eagerly and consistently move toward Jesus.

The reality is that we must learn who we are in Christ, and who he is in us, before we will be able to know what we are called to do for his kingdom. Our calling is a call of action. However, if we do not learn to spend time with him and learn to be like him, we will never fully be able to tap into our potential in ministering for him. We must be with him before we can learn to do ministry for him. If we are called to do anything for God, then we must be ready to live out our calling in ministry for him. Dietrich Bonhoeffer was a German pastor and theologian during the time of Hitler. He lived his life in opposition to the Nazi regime, and eventually died by hanging in a concentration camp because of his stance. Bonhoeffer said:

> [God's call] had everything to do with living one's life in obedience . . . through action. It did not merely require a mind, but a body too. It was God's call to be fully human, to live as human beings obedient to the one who had made us, which was the

fulfillment of our destiny. It was not a cramped, compromised, circumspect life, but a life lived in a kind of wild, joyful, full-throated freedom—that was what is was to obey God.[17]

Our obedience to God means we live life to the fullest and give wholeheartedly to the ministry God has called us to do—we live for him and speak for him unashamedly!

What Process Has God Used To Impact You?

Scanning your life history, how have you seen God work in your life? Obviously, parents, guardians and family play a large part of God's guidance in life—especially during the early years. Through the daily grind in their lives, the struggles they faced, their love for the Lord or lack of knowledge about God, and the way they raised you, each and every detail has had a profound impact on the outcome of your life. In multiple ways, those around you have greatly influenced your early, developmental years. Even if it is difficult to say in every situation, all the experiences in your life—the good, the bad, and the ugly—have shaped the person you are today.

It was interesting to see God work through many situations and circumstances in my life. I learned valuable lessons through various people that God put in my pathway. There were teachers in school, coaches on the field or court, adults in the church, and even friends along the way who spoke into my life. Many of them shared about God's provision; some of them shared testimonies of God's grace and mercy. A few of them told me about challenging lessons learned in a difficult manner. But all of them confirmed the leading of God in every situation—the good and the bad times, the rough and the simple experiences, the ups and downs on the roller-coaster of life. People in your life will build relationships that will help confirm God's call and keep you focused on the prize ahead.

Some of the best and the worst of your life lessons may come through the difficult circumstances of life. We all must learn to deal with relationships, and dealing with people is not always pleasant. In going through trying times, we learn to live life and trust in God. There might be an occasional death in the family or a tragic situation with which to deal. Sometimes, the classroom might be tough. Sometimes, life can be harsh. There will be good days and bad days. Success in life can be sweet, but failure in life can be

17. Metaxas, *Bonhoeffer*, 446.

debilitating at times. So, we must learn to take the bumps and the curves in the road as they came at us. We must learn to keep moving forward, even when life is not pleasant. In fact, it is often those most unpleasant times that will produce, in us, the most amazing results.

Potential Hindrances

So that is the end of the story—we love Jesus and he loves us! We will ride into the sunset of ministry together, right? Unfortunately, a life of service and ministry is not always easy. Just as we learn to engage life growing up through difficulties one day at a time, we must learn to deal with the difficulties of life in ministry. We might not drive the nicest car or live in the most luxurious homes. We will have to work hard to provide for our family, sometimes working a second job just to pay the bills. Our family may not be able to travel to plush locations on vacation; rather, we might be found leading mission trips or attending youth camps. There may be times in our lives that we want to do things or go places, but we do not have the money or the time due to our responsibilities in ministry.

We also need to be careful about other issues that will keep us from moving forward in ministry. Sin is a dangerous temptation for all of us. It has been said that "Sin will take you farther than you want to go, keep you longer than you want to stay and cost you more than you want to pay."[18] Not only will sin affect us, our choices and decisions will greatly influence our success of failure in ministry. What we say on social media, our views about politics, and our comments about people may be full of truth, but we may cause derision that will prevent us from serving in ministry.

A life of ministry means that we are called to a higher standard of living. It means that we are called to sacrifice in life beyond what others might be called on to do. It means that our priority must focus more on God and less on life. The bottom line is that it means that we must live differently, because we are called to minister for God and his kingdom.

You may be uncertain as to what God has called you to do in life. In reality, that is perfectly normal. We do not always have the appropriate leading in life when we want it. Daily, we live and make choices that propel us along our path of life. Those choices are guided by experiences and

18. Although this is a frequently quoted saying, there is no clear origin of this quote. Many preachers and teachers have used this phrase to refer to the dangers of falling to the temptations of sin.

events along the way. Ministry becomes a place of involvement where we can grow in God's grace and learn what it means to work for his kingdom. If we cannot find the "perfect" place of ministry, we should not see that as a problem. In fact, we should focus on living out a dynamic call to ministry, rather than a call that is static or unchanging.[19] God can teach us through every ministry opportunity and bring us along in our ministry continuum.

He can utilize every ministry endeavor to help strengthen our ministry potential and draw us closer to the place where we are supposed to fulfill his purpose for our life. But we have to pay attention to the hurdles and roadblocks along life's journey if we want to serve in ministry.

Conclusion

When I was thinking about going into ministry, my dad sat me down and had a very serious conversation with me. Dad told me that he had learned everything he knew about ministry through the school of "hard knocks and knee-ology." He told me about many of the ups and downs of his ministry life. He shared with me that I would have some good times and some tough times if I decided to go into ministry. And then, he made a statement that I will never forget—a statement that I often use when talking with students or young people going into ministry. Dad said, "Son, if you can do anything with your life other than ministry and be happy—please do it! But if you cannot do anything with your life other than ministry, then do ministry with all your might!"

In over fifty-four years of ministry, Dad has had many ups and downs, but he has held on to God through his roller-coaster ride in ministry. Likewise, I have had many good days and many bad days in thirty-five years of ministry, but I have held on to God through every situation and circumstance. Even though life has been tough at times, I can tell you without reservation that I must do ministry. I cannot change course; I cannot quit; I cannot do anything other than ministry. God has called me, and I must follow him wherever he leads me.

Toward the end of his first letter, Peter encouraged his readers to keep working because the end was near. He reassured them that God would be with them through every situation:

19. Cross, *Answering the Call*, 2.

Each of you should use whatever gift you have received to serve others, as faithful stewards of God's grace in its various forms. If anyone speaks, they should do so as one who speaks the very words of God. If anyone serves, they should do so with the strength God provides, so that in all things God may be praised through Jesus Christ. To him be the glory and the power for ever and ever. Amen. (1 Pet 4:10–11)

If you are reading this text, there is a good possibility that you are contemplating giving your life to ministry. If God has called you, follow him and do not give up in your fight to love and serve others on behalf of your Savior. Give God your all and do what you can do to positively impact your world for the sake of Christ. If God has called you, whatever you do in life, he will be with you!

Questions for Reflection

1. Does your current life setting or context represent a life you are passionate about?

2. How can you develop what you are passionate about to help bring meaning and depth to the lives of those around you?

3. What gifts, talents, abilities, and experiences has God placed in your life that will help you find your calling and help you impact others through that calling?

4. What is the purpose your calling will help you live out in your life?

5. Who is God calling you to be, and what is God calling you to do with your life?

For Further Reading

Cross, Terry L. *Answering the Call in the Spirit: Pentecostal Reflections on a Theology of Vocation, Work, and Life*. Cleveland, TN: Lee University, 2002.

Groeschel, Craig. *Divine Direction: 7 Decisions That Will Change Your Life*. Grand Rapids: Zondervan Publishing House, 2017.

Piper, John. *Don't Waste Your Life*. Wheaton, IL: Crossway Books, 2007.

Platt, David. *Counter Culture: Following Christ in an Anti-Christian Age*. Carol Stream, Illinois: Tyndale House Publishers, 2017.

Volf, Miroslav. *A Public Faith: How Followers of Christ Should Serve the Common Good*. Grand Rapids: Brazos, 2011.

The Priority of Leadership

Mark L. Walker, PhD[1]

To aspire to leadership is an honorable ambition.

—1 Tim 3:1 (NEB)

My dream as a small boy was to be the leader of a large corporation in a major city occupying a large office suite atop a towering downtown skyscraper overlooking the city skyline. The idea of leading a big business intrigued me. Three years into my business career, I realized that my dream was not about leading a major company. The dream was about being a leader—specifically, a pastoral leader. The organization God wanted me to lead was his church. Doors opened by his hand, and I found myself living the dream. And, for over thirty years, God allowed me the amazing privilege to serve as a pastoral leader.

If I learned anything as a pastoral leader, it is that leadership is a huge responsibility and it must be made a priority. Good leadership is not something that just happens: it is intentional. Effective leaders make leadership a priority. The Apostle Paul makes this clear to Timothy when he writes, "To aspire to leadership is an honorable ambition" (1 Tim 3:1, NEB), and we

---

1. Mark Walker serves as the Vice President for Ministerial Development and the Chair of the Department of Christian Ministries at Lee University. He is a professor of Pastoral Studies, and he holds a Doctor of Philosophy degree in Organizational Leadership from Regent University. His ministry includes over thirty years of pastoral leadership, twenty-five of which were at Mount Paran North Church of God in Marietta, Georgia. Walker has served on various committees and councils at the highest levels of leadership in the Church of God denomination. He and his wife, Udella, have two married children and two grandchildren.

hear Christ's intentionality in his words to Peter: "Come, follow Me, and I will make you fishers of men" (Mark 1:17).[2] Leadership is a priority.

Bill Hybels states that the church will not achieve its full redemptive potential until those entrusted with leadership step up and exercise their leadership calling.[3] George Barna furthers this idea by writing that Christian leaders have the most influence on society because their "leadership affects the visible presence of God and His ways in our world."[4] For me, the priority of pastoral leadership is to lead churches in such a way that the full force of the redemptive message of Christ is unleashed in the Earth. But what is the priority of such leadership?

When Christ began his public ministry, his major leadership priority was to make disciples (Matt 4:18–22; Mark 1:14–20; 2:13–14; Luke 5:1–11, 27–31; John 1:35–51). Wherever he went teaching, preaching, healing, performing miracles, and building relationships, he invited people to follow him. Then he closed his time on Earth by commissioning these same disciples to follow his example and make disciples (Matt 28:18–20; Mark 16:15–17; Luke 24:47–48; John 20:21; Acts 1:8). Disciple-making was Christ's priority for his followers and, therefore, must be the priority of leadership for his pastoral leaders.

Everything a church does must align with Christ's Great Commission to the church.[5] Pastoral leaders and their churches cannot make a significant difference unless they are individually and corporately sold out to Christ and his commission to "go and make disciples" (Matt 28:20). The priority of pastoral leadership is to lead disciple-making churches!

Defining Terms

In this chapter, the term "pastoral leader" is not exclusive to lead pastors, but identifies anyone, paid staff or volunteer, who is serving in any pastoral leadership role in the church. Leadership occurs at all levels of an organization. Research shows that the leader who has the most influence on a person's day-to-day performance is the leader to whom he/she directly

2. All Scripture quotations are from the New International Version (NIV) unless otherwise noted.

3. Hybels, *Courageous Leadership*, 27.

4. Barna, *Fish Out of Water*, xxiv.

5. See Tom Doolittle's previous chapter.

reports.[6] Whatever their position, good leaders can turn their areas of responsibility into "pockets of greatness."[7] Although the lead pastor is the primary person to lead the way in the leadership practices required for a church to be an effective disciple-making church, all leaders at all levels must partner with the lead pastor to perform these practices throughout the church.

Through my study of pastoral leadership, the many conversations I have had with other pastoral leaders, and the trials and errors of my own experiences as a pastoral leader, I see five leadership practices that must be a priority for leading an effective disciple-making church: casting vision, communicating values, creating systems, caring for people, and committing to personal discipleship. Thus, for this chapter, a pastoral leader is anyone serving in any pastoral leadership role performing these priorities.

Casting Vision

Vision casting seems to be more of an art than a science. Browsing church publications and websites reveals an abundance of church vision statements. Although vision is not a one-size-fits-all proposition, it contains some common features essential to its effectiveness. For instance, vision creates a picture of the future. Some have used terms like "God-driven picture of success;"[8] "view of the future;"[9] "forward-looking;"[10] "picture of the future;"[11] and "the big picture."[12] A second feature common to a vision is that it compels people to participate: "Willing to die for;"[13] "produces passion;"[14] "stirs hearts and minds;"[15] "focuses on the exciting

---

6. Kouzes and Posner, *Truth About Leadership*, 11.

7. Scroggins, *How to Lead*, 29.

8. Lovejoy, *Be Mean About The Vision*, 25.

9. Blanchard and Hodges, *Lead Like Jesus*, 88.

10. Kouzes and Posner, *Truth About Leadership*, 46.

11. Hybels, *Courageous Leadership*, 32.

12. Hull, *Disciple-Making Pastor*, 134.

13. Lovejoy, *Be Mean About The Vision*, 39.

14. Hybels, *Courageous Leadership*, 32.

15. Blanchard and Hodges, *Lead Like Jesus*, 88.

possibilities;"[16] and "where a group is going"[17] are terms used to describe how vision motivates people to action.

Christ painted a gripping picture of the future reign of his kingdom on the Earth. He called people to repent and believe in him because the kingdom was near, and he wanted them to be a part of it (Matt 4:17; Mark 1:15). Through parables, Christ painted a visual portrait of his kingdom. Christ used images like wheat and weeds (Matt 13:24–30); mustard seed and yeast (13:31–33); hidden treasure (13:34); a pearl (13:35); a fishing net (13:47–52); a wedding banquet (21:33–44); sheep and goats (25:31–46) and more. He spoke of his coming eternal kingdom and how those who followed him were guaranteed a place in it (16:27–28; Mark 10:29–31; Luke 22:28–30; John 3:16). In the context of motivating people to be his disciples, Christ effectively cast a vision of the preferred future of his kingdom—a vision so compelling that people were willing to leave everything and follow him (Matt 4:20–22; Mark 2:14).

Research indicates that there appears to be a significant connection between vision-casting and disciple-making. For example, Willow Creek Community Church conducted a worldwide survey entitled REVEAL. The study indicated that the number-one pastoral leadership quality that seemed to generate the greatest desire within people to grow spiritually was preaching and vision-casting that encouraged spiritual growth as a priority of life.[18] In another study, the Barna Research Group focused on twenty-four churches that were highly effective in making disciples.[19] One finding was that the pastor's main function in disciple-making was expressing a passionate vision that motivated the congregation to engage in their own personal spiritual growth and the growth of others. Vision-casting is a critical priority of pastoral leadership.

There are two important elements about vision-casting that pastoral leaders should keep in mind. One, vision begins with a burden. Two, vision leaks. As an example, the leadership story of Nehemiah has always been one of my favorites. When he heard that the Jerusalem walls had been torn down by Babylon and that the Israelites were living unprotected and in disgrace, Nehemiah "sat down and wept" (Neh 1:4). He was burdened for them. Vision is birthed out of a burden. Highly successful disciple-making

16. Kouzes and Posner, *Truth About Leadership*, 58.

17. Hull, *Disciple-Making Pastor*, 134.

18. Hawkins and Parkinson, *Focus*, 72.

19. Barna, *Growing True Disciples*, 105.

pastoral leader Shawn Lovejoy calls it "holy discontentment."[20] God placed a holy discontentment in Nehemiah and compelled him to do something about it. The vision that has the greatest potential for success is one that has emerged from a God-given burden. Pastoral leaders of effective Great Commission churches have a vision driven by some type of holy discontentment to make disciples of Christ.

It has been said many times that vision leaks. In other words, people tend to forget an organization's vision if they do not hear it over and over again. Everyday, people are overloaded with so much information that the vision of the church often leaks from the forefront of their thinking. I discovered that when I was tired of talking about the vision, the people were just starting to remember it. Leaders can never cast the vision enough. Effective vision-casting takes the constant utilization of all communication platforms—sermons, social media, websites, small groups, conversations, publications, etc. To overcome people losing sight of the vision, there is no limit as to how often and by what means the vision should be cast. Pastoral leaders must make it a priority to paint the picture over and over again of what people's lives, families, communities, workplaces, and cities will look like as they follow Christ.

Communicating Values

As pastoral leaders cast a disciple-making vision, they also communicate the core values of what constitutes making disciples. Core values are the non-negotiable elements that shape the vision and make it possible to achieve. From a biblical perspective, pastoral leaders have to answer this question: what is a disciple? Otherwise, how does anyone know if the vision is being accomplished?

People view their pastoral leaders as the lead Bible communicators and experts of the church.[21] They expect and trust their pastoral leaders to teach and preach accurate truths of Scripture. A primary function of pastoral leaders is to study, understand, and articulate the Scriptures in a way that people can grasp and apply their meaning (2 Tim 2:15). Teaching God's word was fundamental to Christ's disciple-making ministry (Matt 4:23; 5:2; 7:28–29; Mark 6:34; Luke 4:15; 5:3; John 3:2; 7:14; 8:2). In fact, Christ's teaching amazed his hearers and set him apart from all other teach-

20. Lovejoy, *Be Mean About The Vision*, 21.
21. Hawkins and Parkinson, *Focus*, 57.

ers (Matt 7:28–29; Mark 1:21–22). Scriptural teaching is so vital to making disciples that Christ included it as a major aspect of the Great Commission (Matt 28:20).

Pastoral leaders of Great Commission churches are devoted to becoming master Bible communicators. They must be lifetime Bible students who strive to passionately and accurately teach and preach sound doctrine in a relevant manner. In so doing, pastoral leaders not only grow disciples; they create within their churches a relevant and sound Bible-teaching culture that is highly conducive to making disciples. Yet, such Bible teaching is not only essential to growing disciples—it is also essential to communicating the vision's core values of being and making disciples.

For pastoral leaders to define the core values of discipleship, they must begin with the scriptural meaning of disciple-making. The Great Commission's key phrase, "make disciples," means the "deep shaping of character and the cultivation of a worldview through a close personal relationship between the disciple and the master or leader."[22] Disciple-making is much more than acquiring knowledge, attaining information, or developing a skill; it is about a follower being transformed by the values and beliefs of the teacher in the context of a committed and growing fellowship with the teacher.[23] Making disciples goes beyond just gathering people together for weekend worship services; instead, it is developing followers who accept the instructions and lifestyle of Jesus Christ as a way of life.

Articulating a scriptural foundation for making disciples is the starting place for communicating the core values of a disciple. If the church's vision is rooted in disciple-making, then it is crucial for pastoral leaders to know and communicate the biblical core essentials of a disciple. Pastoral leaders have to establish what a disciple of Christ looks like if the church is going to effectively develop them. Without it, the church and their pastoral leaders never know where they are in the vision.

For example, perhaps a church describes disciples as people who live Christ-centered lives. Their vision statement could read something like, "We are here to help the people of our community and around the world discover and live a Christ-centered life." Then the pastoral leadership has to determine the non-negotiable values for what constitutes a Christ-centered life (a disciple). These core essentials become the tracks upon which the

22. Zodhiates, *Hebrew Greek*, 1647.
23. Zodhiates, *Hebrew Greek*, 1647.

vision runs. They are earmarks for measuring the pace and the success of helping people discover and live Christ-centered lives.

Pastoral leaders should be aware, however, that determining the core values of the vision is not necessarily an easy task. It takes time, prayer, study and dialogue with others. The values must align with the vision and uphold the scriptural understanding of making disciples. Values must be communicated in an easy to understand way and should be simple, yet challenging. Such a task may appear daunting, but it is essential and can be done. Being alone with God in prayer, studying God's word, and spending time discussing insights and ideas with other leaders are fundamental to the process for determining the core values of discipleship. Pastoral leaders have no choice if they are going to lead fully functioning disciple-making churches.

Creating Systems

Perhaps the most neglected piece of pastoral leadership in leading a Great Commission church is the design of systems and processes that strategically help people move through the core values of being a disciple. Just as Christ appeared to move his disciples through an intentional growth path, pastoral leaders should do the same, and design a sequential, next-step process that helps people move through the core values, calling them to greater levels of commitment at each phase of the process.

Christ's disciple-making approach implied a process of movement toward deeper commitment and growth from his followers.[24] For example, Christ began by engaging people in their daily lives and then personally invited them to follow him (Luke 5). After spending all night in prayer, Christ appointed twelve to be his apostles, officially establishing them as his called disciples (Luke 6). Christ then exposed them to opportunities designed to develop their faith. He taught them of the kingdom (Luke 7) and allowed them to observe him minister to people in the power, grace and love of the kingdom (Luke 8). In the next phase of their discipleship, Christ sent his followers out to do what they had seen and heard him do and teach. It appears that Christ had a strategically designed disciple-making process that intentionally moved his followers toward greater spiritual development and devotion.

The idea is for churches, without any wasted ministry energy or effort, to make disciples in accordance with their articulated vision and

24. Rainer and Geiger, *Simple Church*, 161.

communicated values. The Barna Research Group's study of twenty-four highly effective disciple-making churches revealed that churches failed at making disciples when they attempted to produce disciples without a well-defined compelling definition of discipleship and without a clear long-term disciple-making plan that drove ministry implementation.[25] The research also indicated that churches were more successful at developing disciples when they redesigned or eliminated ministries that did not support their disciple-making strategy.[26] Churches that had a definite plan of growth that was simple, yet challenging, were more likely to do well at making disciples.

Good stewardship of God's resources and people's time demand that pastoral leaders diligently establish ministries and systems that effectively and efficiently disciple their people. Results from the REVEAL study showed that the leadership of the pastor, rather than the teaching of the pastor, was far more influential on people's satisfaction with the church's role in their spiritual growth.[27] The study's definition of pastoral leadership included the phrase "provides a clear pathway that helps guide my spiritual growth."[28] The teaching of the pastor was defined as providing sound doctrine, challenging people to spiritually grow and take next steps, and modeling personal spiritual development.

People want and need sound teaching from their pastoral leaders. Even more so, people need their pastoral leaders to make the strategic and sometimes-tough choices of leadership that reflect the disciple-making vision and values of the church. Such decisions would include hiring and firing staff, starting new ministries and ending non-productive ones, and allocating and cutting resources, all for the purpose of designing clear pathways that move people into and through the strategically designed process of discipleship. Helping people move toward and through the church's disciple-making vision and values is an ongoing function of pastoral leadership. Ministries and systems must constantly be assessed to make sure they are effectively contributing to the process of discipleship. Ministries sometimes lose their focus and need recalibrating. They sometimes run their course and must be shut down. Such a leadership process can be painful at times and requires godly wisdom, discernment, and timing. Some ministries may be sacred to a pocket of people, yet they no longer serve to

25. Barna, *Growing True Disciples*, 119.
26. Barna, *Growing True Disciples*, 128.
27. Hawkins and Parkinson, *Focus*, 81.
28. Hawkins and Parkinson, *Focus*, 78.

help people grow or move in the core values of discipleship. Changing or eliminating these ministries may require a great deal of patience and tact. Continually casting the church's disciple-making vision and communicating the church's core values of discipleship is vital to helping bring about such changes. If the people involved in ministries that require change or elimination can catch and own the vision and values, then they often make the needed change on their own.

Regardless of the potential challenges ministry adjustments may bring, pastoral leaders cannot neglect the leadership priority of creating and maintaining the systems, processes, and ministries that help people grow and move in the core values of discipleship. People are trusting their pastoral leadership to help them fully develop as disciples of Christ, and they not only need a vision and values to pursue, but they need a strategically designed path to take them there. They want their pastoral leaders to point the way.

Caring for People

Big visions, lofty values, and strategic systems mean little to nothing unless a sincere care for people is at the heart. Pastoral leadership is not about building great empires of power, but about serving people. Christ's whole personal model of leadership and the model to which he called his followers was "not to be served, but to serve" (Matt 20:25–28; Mark 10:42–45). He had compassion for people, as he would often see them as "sheep without a shepherd" (Matthew 9:36; Mark 6:34). There was no human need beneath Christ, as he beautifully demonstrated when he washed his disciples' feet (John 13:1–17). Of course, Christ's greatest act of selfless love for humanity was his willing death on a cross: "Greater love has no one than this: to lay down one's life for one's friends" (John 15:13).

Disciple-making pastoral leaders love people. Unless the vison, values, and systems are motivated by a genuine care for people, then people will not care for the vision, values, and systems. They will not follow leadership. Although it has been said *ad nauseum*, it is worth repeating: "people do not care how much you know until they know how much you care." According to John Maxwell, when leaders show a genuine desire to take care of their followers' needs, they earn the right to be followed.[29] He offers four ways that have often served as reminders to me that care is key. One, instead of

---

29. Maxwell. *21 Most Powerful Minutes in a Leader's Day.*

lecturing, listen. Two, instead of projecting image, project integrity. Three, instead of demanding control, demonstrate compassion. Four, instead of glaring at others, gaze through their eyes.[30]

In their research on the qualities that motivate people to follow exemplary leaders, James M. Kouzes and Barry Z. Posner discovered that the best leaders are those who are the most open and caring.[31] Compared to low-performing leaders, high-performing leaders show greater affection for their followers and demonstrate greater love and compassion. They are not the center of attention; rather, they place their followers there. They do not seek to meet their own interests first; instead, they respond to the interests and needs of their followers.[32] In short, exemplary leaders are more concerned about leaving a lasting legacy than they are about becoming a legend.[33]

Pastoral leaders care, because they want people to follow. They want people to follow, because they want people to become disciples of Jesus Christ. They want people to become disciples of Jesus Christ, because it is the greatest human need on Earth. There is no greater way to love people than to show them Christ's way. Vision, values, and systems are driven by a genuine care for people to encounter Jesus Christ. Disciple-making pastoral leaders love people!

Committing to Personal Discipleship

The greatest disciple to ever live was Jesus Christ. He followed God the Father and did his will (John 4:34). He spoke only what his Father wanted him to speak (John 7:16–17). He spent countless hours in prayer with his Father (Mark 1:35; 6:46–47; Luke 5:15–16; 6:12). He lived to please and glorify the Father (John 8:28–29; 12:25–28; 14:13). Christ modeled to his followers the discipleship life to which he called them. He did not just make disciples—he was one. He made personal discipleship a priority. Christ, the ultimate disciple-maker, was a disciple.

Some of my favorite leadership authors contend that modeling is the most important leadership function in making disciples. For example, Kouzes and Posner found in their research that credibility is what people want most in a leader, and the number-one leadership practice that builds

30. Maxwell. *21 Most Powerful Minutes in a Leader's Day*, 161.

31. Kouzes and Posner, *Truth About Leadership*, 136.

32. Kouzes and Posner, *Truth About Leadership*, 138.

33. Kouzes and Posner, *Truth About Leadership*, 140.

credibility is leading by example.[34] Hull states that, after teaching the way of discipleship, modeling the way is the most effective teacher.[35] Hybels insists that the most forceful way pastoral leaders can get their vision across is "By embodying it. By personifying it. By living it out."[36] Rainer and Geiger claim that pastors living and doing what they have asked others to live and do is a matter of integrity—it is the difference between pastoral leaders being spiritual travel agents and spiritual tour guides.[37] Travel agents provide great information about nice places to travel. They send brochures and encourage people to have an exciting journey, but that is as far as travel agents go. Tour guides do not just talk about the journey; they join in the journey. They participate and lead the way

The Apostle Paul best captured the importance of modeling the way of discipleship when he wrote to the Corinthian church: "Follow my example, as I follow the example of Christ" (1 Cor 11:1). He also reminded the Thessalonians that his leadership team worked to make a living while they were with them to serve as a model of behavior for those who were idle (2 Thess 3:9). Paul further instructed his protégés, Timothy and Titus, to serve as models of discipleship to their followers (1 Tim 4:12; Titus 2:7).

Pastoral leaders must be disciples first before they can be effective disciple-makers. They are their church's top models of the disciple-making vision they cast, values they communicate, systems they create, and people for which they care. They must be active visual participants in the defined disciple-making process of the church, which means if one of the church's discipleship core values is defined as being in community with others in small groups, then pastoral leaders need to be a part of a small group. If being a witness is a core value defined as building relationships with unbelievers, then the pastoral leaders should be seeking to build relationships with unbelievers. Pastoral leaders that launch disciple-making visions and values must be committed to living out the very vision and values they espouse. The research of Kouzes and Posner tells the story: "you either lead by example or you don't lead at all."[38]

Unfortunately, the leadership landscape is riddled with fallen pastoral leaders, and many times it is because they failed to be disciples before they

---

34. Kouzes and Posner, *Truth About Leadership*, 106.

35. Hull, *Disciple-Making Pastor*, 251.

36. Hybels, *Courageous Leadership*, 38.

37. Rainer and Geiger, *Simple Church*, 132.

38. Kouzes and Posner, *Truth About Leadership*, 106.

were anything else. I am God's son first, before I am his pastoral leader. I am to pursue God, not perform for him. God called me to pastoral leadership; God made me to be his child. My pastoral leadership is temporary; my relationship with Jesus Christ is eternal. For my own sake, I must be committed to my own personal discipleship, not just for the sake of making disciples. Without it, I lose my way as a person and a leader. The most important reason for pastoral leaders to model personal discipleship is for the development and preservation of their own souls, not just the souls of their church.

Conclusion

If Christ is the answer for the world, then pastoral leaders must lead in such a way that the church is unleashed as Christ's full disciple-making force in the Earth. Pastoral leaders cannot lead churches to their full disciple-making potential unless they are individually and corporately sold out to Christ and his Great Commission. Like Christ, the ultimate disciple-maker, the priority of pastoral leaders is to cast a vision, communicate values, create systems, care for people, and be committed to personal discipleship. The priority of the Great Commission must drive how, why, and to what end pastoral leaders lead.

Questions for Reflection

1. Which of the five pastoral leadership practices do you most connect to? Least connect to? Why?

2. What are some ways you would keep vision from leaking?

3. What are some core biblical values essential to making disciples?

4. What are some systems that would help people move on a path of discipleship?

5. What are some ways pastoral leaders can demonstrate genuine care for people?

6. How important is it for pastoral leaders to model personal discipleship?

For Further Reading

Chand, Sam. *Bigger, Faster Leadership: Lessons from the Builders of the Panama Canal.* Nashville: Thomas Nelson, 2017.

———. *Leadership Pain: The Classroom for Growth.* Nashville: Thomas Nelson, 2015.

Isaacs, Jeremy and Jason Isaacs. *Toxic Soul: A Pastor's Guide to Leading Without Losing Heart.* Canton, GA: Self-published, 2017.

Lomenick, Brad. *H3 Leadership: Be Humble. Stay Hungry. Always Hustle.* Nashville: Thomas Nelson, 2015.

Lovejoy, Shawn. *The Measure of Our Success: An Impassioned Plea to Pastors.* Grand Rapids: Baker, 2012.

The Urgency of Evangelism

Bill Effler, DMin[1]

We must work the works of him who sent me while it is day;
night is coming when no one can work.

—JOHN 9:4[2]

A PERSON WHOSE LIFE is governed by a sense of urgency sees an opportunity they think they can seize and takes action. Persons who are a cut above the rest attempt more and achieve more; equally, these persons are not easily derailed by disappointment, but rather choose to chart their lives by way of resiliency and urgency. Today's adrenaline-driven and entitlement-based culture is not founded or grounded on urgency. Rather than hearing "Let's get this done now," we more commonly hear, "Yes, but . . . how about tomorrow?"

---

1. Dr. Bill Effler received his undergraduate degree from the *University of Southern California*, and both graduate and postgraduate degrees from *Fuller Theological Seminary*. As an ordained Presbyterian minister (PCUSA), he served four churches in a variety of capacities, including that of senior pastor. He has been an intake counselor in a residential treatment facility, a case counselor in a group practice, and consults with churches and businesses in the non-profit sector, including the Southeastern Tennessee Alzheimer's Association, where he was a board member. Since 2000, he has been on the faculty in the School of Religion at Lee University in Cleveland, Tennessee, where he teaches courses in the Pastoral Studies area. Bill's previously published work includes *Turning the Church Inside Out* and *Out From the Shadows: Biblical Counseling Revealed in the Story of Creation*. He and his wife Kristen reside in southeast Tennessee, and are the parents of three grown children.

2. All Scripture quotations are from the New Revised Standard Version (NRSV) unless otherwise noted.

For many years now, I have noticed a lack of urgency in the way self-professing Christians approach what might be termed "evangelistic opportunities." Whether it is in my home state of California or in the state of Tennessee where I have lived the last sixteen years, there is a developed passivity and reluctance among believers to share anything that God has done in their lives. Some churchgoers prefer a toned-down message of the gospel that could be described as inimically conversational, rather than a presentation of the gospel that would invite a person to question their own worldview. This contemporary shift from an urgency in evangelism as found in Scripture to a lethargic response about evangelism as found in today's culture troubles me greatly.

Thomas Rainer, in a recent Twitter poll, identified fifteen reasons why churches today are less evangelistic than as seen in recent history. Heading the list, says Rainer, is that "Christians have *no sense of urgency* to reach lost people."[3] Rainer substantiates this observation in the context of his own church by saying, "By almost any metric, the churches in the nation are much less evangelistic today than they were in the recent past. . . .we are reaching non-Christians only half as effectively as we were fifty years ago."[4] Two ideas on Rainer's list of fifteen that are not customarily cited include the following: many churches have unregenerate members who have not received Christ themselves, and some churches have theological systems in place that simply do not encourage the ministry of evangelism![5]

My Journey towards Urgency

As a new follower of Christ, I was given specific instruction and mentoring, as well as clear encouragement and practical direction that I needed a greater sense of urgency. My college pastor[6] taught classes on the spiritual disciplines.[7] Pastor Al also modeled what could be called relational evange-

---

3. Rainer, "Fifteen Reasons," para. 1. Emphasis added.

4. Rainer, "Fifteen Reasons," para. 1.

5. Rainer, "Fifteen Reasons," para. 5.

6. I am so very thankful for Dr. Al Stones, who took the necessary time to encourage a very insecure kid. I have come to know that insecurity marks many young men's lives. Because of my own deeper healing through the years, I intentionally seek to encourage the young men I meet in the university where I teach.

7. See Richard Foster's classic work, *Celebration of Discipline: The Path to Spiritual Growth*; first published in 1978, the book is referred to as a Christian classic on the subject of Christian spirituality.

lism.[8] These two expressions of the Christian life, evangelism and discipleship, were shared with equal importance; neither expression of Christian living was taught as a programmatic add-on, or as some academic elective that was viewed as optional. Two years after my conversion experience, my home church sent me to Seoul, Korea on a summer mission experience. Joined by two other guys from my college department, whose names were also Bill (yes, our Korean friends were confused and amused!), my passion for evangelism was ignited. In later years I came to understand the discipleship principle that "people grow to go, and then go to grow further."[9] In looking back on my home church's emphasis on evangelism, it does not surprise me today that evangelism would eventually become a high priority for me in later years.

For decades, the church of my youth intentionally aligned itself with significant pioneers in the ministry of evangelism, church planting and cross cultural ministry. My parent's college pastor, Henrietta Mears, was in many ways ahead of her time as an evangelist, entrepreneur, curriculum developer, and charismatic leader. She was a "national big deal" for her time. Her ministry attracted hundreds of college students on a weekly basis from all over the greater southern California area. During a time that we now refer to as the Baby Boomer era, Mears was asked by a young and then-unknown evangelist, Billy Graham, to help promote his first tent revival meeting in downtown Hollywood, California.[10] The rest, you can say, is history.

Bill Bright,[11] founder of Campus Crusade for Christ (an international evangelistic ministry on college campuses, worldwide), was one of "Teach-

8. Relational evangelism is a specific recognized approach to sharing the good news of the gospel with another person by first establishing a relationship with a person before ever sharing Scripture or anything that may be construed as "religious in nature." There are both positive and undesirable aspects of this approach to evangelism.

9. Dr. Gary Sweeten taught what many of us have come to know: there are some lessons that simply cannot be taught or learned in the classroom.

10. Billy Graham's first crusade lasted eight weeks and encompassed seventy-two meetings. Graham attributes his clarity of vision to time spent with Mears at her conference ground, Forest Home.

11. Bright's evangelistic college ministry began on the campus of UCLA using "four spiritual laws" as his guiding approach to evangelism. Today, Campus Crusade has more than twenty thousand full-time staff in 181 countries. Other evangelistic ministries that were spawned directly out of Bright's influence include Josh McDowell Ministries, Athletes in Action, and the Jesus Film project. To learn more about collegiate evangelistic ministers, go to www.cru.com.

er Mear's boys," greatly influenced by his college pastor. The contributions of Bright's ministry are still felt today, and are the direct result of a church that saw the importance of instilling the passion of evangelism in the lives of young people. During the 1980s, I benefitted from the pulpit ministry of Lloyd John Ogilvie and his corresponding television ministry, "Let God Love You." With the dawning of a new day in television, Ogilvie's biblical, transparent, and practical preaching was used as a national evangelistic and publishing tool. Later, Ogilvie would become a clear voice of evangelism as the chaplain of the United States Senate. In one respect, this church infused me with a newfound evangelistic DNA. I pause to say, sadly, that the days of intentional evangelistic training and education in the local church that are described here are gone. The question this chapter seeks to answer is this: "How can a sense of urgency for the ministry of evangelism that was once held in such high regard be recaptured?" The first step in regaining anything that is lost is to recognize that it is missing in the first place. In the pages that follow, I offer my own subsequent steps to regaining lost evangelistic urgency by identifying (1) the evangelistic urgency in the life of Jesus, (2) challenges to evangelistic urgency found in contemporary culture, and (3) the importance of evangelistic urgency in pulpit ministry today.

Evangelistic Urgency in the Life and Ministry of Jesus

Luke chapter 9 begins with the calling, giving, empowering and sending out of the disciples (vv. 1–2) to the mission field of their day. These two verses offer one description of the calling of evangelists.[12] It is interesting to observe that in the following chapter, Luke 10, we find a refrain or echo to Luke 9. However, what is found in chapter 10 is marked with a greater degree of urgency. In Luke 10, Jesus says, "The harvest is plentiful, but the laborers are few" (10:2). This verse tells why the ministry of evangelism is to be marked by urgency. The ministry of evangelism is a matter of urgency because so few would-be Christians participate in this ministry. Any Christian without a sense of evangelistic urgency is nothing more than a "poser"; that is to say, not a real Christian. In the next verse, Jesus commands, "Go on your way." This command is the "when" of evangelistic urgency. When Jesus says "move out," the troops move out! Do you not hear the urgency in this edict?

12. Each of these four words, easily, are individually full of significance and worthy of further individual reflection.

Returning to Luke 9, we hear a very clear prohibition to Jesus' followers, as evidenced in the words "Take nothing" (9:3–4). These verses seem to imply that the evangelist's life is to be marked by simplicity. Jesus' instructions continue in a very practical, yet cautionary, way, as he says, "Wherever they do not welcome you, as you are leaving that town shake the dust off your feet" (9:5). With this instruction, Jesus seems to be saying, "Do not loiter in a place that is not receptive to my message." In verse 6, following Jesus' brief instructions, Luke simply records, "They [the disciples] departed and went through the villages." End of sentence. No further instruction is necessary. No questions are asked by the disciples. The disciples departed, period. Clearly, the disciples had a sense of urgency about them. The chapter continues with Herod's confusion over Jesus' escalating ministry (9:7–9), the feeding of the five thousand (9:10–17), Peter's confession of Jesus as the promised Messiah (9:18–20), and the transfiguration of Jesus on the mountaintop (9:28–29). And then there is more.

Challenges to Evangelistic Urgency Today

After Jesus' return from the mountain with Peter, James, and John, the gospel writer Luke records six specific challenges that prevent or hinder evangelistic urgency (Luke 9:37–62). These challenges are commonly found in our culture today. Evangelistic urgency is hindered any time there is any of the following.

A lack of power

Luke records that the disciples could not exorcise a young boy who was demon-possessed (9:37–40). Their mindset, thinking that they "lack power," is actually commonly found in our day. This sense of spiritual insufficiency is seen regardless of age, gender, educational training, or ministry experience. Christians who say they lack power are believing a lie. This lie comes from the Father of lies,[13] and carries with it a false understanding of the authority that has been given by Jesus to all of his followers.[14]

---

13. John 8:44. This lie, "you can't" or "you are not enough," was first suggested to Eve in Genesis 3:5.

14. Matthew 28:18–19.

A lack of humility

This is reflected in the disciple's argument about who among them would be the greatest (9:46–47). Any time God's servants "jockey for position," (seeking recognition or power) much like jockeys compete in a horserace for the inside rail, the servant of God has lost more than urgency; they have lost the basis from which all priorities come. A loss of humility breeds a loss of teachabilty.

A lack of compassion

Luke records that the disciples want to "command fire to come down from heaven and consume [the Samaritans]" (9:54). A lack of compassion is a third component that dilutes any expression of ministry. A lack of compassion has no place in a believer's life, especially for persons considering the ministry of evangelism.[15]   *James*   *Nigh*

A failure to remember Jesus' previous instructions

If the disciples had "remembered" Jesus' earlier instructions regarding unwelcoming cities ("shake the dust off your feet" in Luke 9:5), the disciples would have simply "moved on." However, they seem to forget this instruction, become offended at their ill treatment, and want to torch the city because of how they were treated. When a follower of Jesus fails to remember their Lord's instructions, there will be trouble ahead.

A lack of commitment

At the end of Luke 9, Luke identifies three different travelers that approach Jesus (9:57–58). Each of the three travelers state that they want to follow Jesus. In the end, none do. In two of the three mini case studies described, the travelers (9:59, 61) offer legitimate reasons why they could not follow Jesus, immediately. Any time there is a lack of commitment to Jesus, there will be legitimized "reasons" as to why one cannot follow. When duplicity enters a disciple's life, urgency is compromised.

15. Kinnaman, *You Lost Me: Why Young Christians Are Leaving Church . . . and Rethinking Faith.* In his book, Kinnaman cites the signature reason why people stay away from Christians today: "Christians are unsafe to be around" (9–14).

Failure to be future-focused

Luke 9 ends with a very serious challenge by Jesus. Hear the following words carefully: "No one who . . . looks back is fit for the kingdom of God" (9:62). There are two classic traps when people "look back" from where they have come. People either romanticize the past, making the past much better than it actually was, or catastrophize the past, and thereby make the past much worse than it really was. In either case, when one falls into this subtle trap, one is no longer forward-looking. Evangelists, by their renewed nature, are forward- or future-oriented persons. The Apostle Paul clearly knew the importance of this principle as he shared with the Philippians, "Beloved, I do not consider that I have made it my own; but this one thing I do: forgetting what lies behind and straining forward to what lies ahead, I press on toward the goal for the prize of the heavenly call of God in Christ Jesus" (Phil 3:13–14).

Any Christian whose life lacks power, humility, compassion, a good memory, commitment, or a future-oriented-ness will have diminished evangelistic urgency. On the other hand, any Christian who has the ability to embrace these very same principles in a constructive way will discover a greater sense of evangelistic urgency. Before reading any further, why not pause now and ask the Lord of the harvest for an impartation of urgency in evangelism, beginning with these six principles?

Evangelistic Urgency in the Pulpits of Yesterday

When thinking about evangelistic urgency in the pulpit, one cannot help but think of Jonathan Edwards and his classic sermon of the Great Awakening, "Sinners in the Hand of an Angry God."[16] This sermon is marked by three evangelistic preaching principles. They are as follows: the exaltation of the person and work of Jesus Christ, the unapologetic demand for behavioral change, and perhaps most notably, the reality of judgment and hell for those who choose to live apart from God. During the same period, Puritan preacher Richard Baxter also modeled a clear sense of evangelistic urgency. Richard Baxter once said, "I preach as never sure to preach again and as a dying man to dying men."[17] Baxter understood that presenting

16. This sermon was preached first to his own congregation in North Hampton, and later on July 8, 1741, in Enfield, Connecticut.

17. Jones and Martin, *Preaching and Preachers*, 85–86.

the gospel message was a matter of life or death. One can be reasonably assured that the urgency of these two reformers of yesterday are absent in the preaching of most pulpits today.

Evangelistic urgency in the pulpit was also clearly seen in the person and ministry of John Knox. It was Knox who was to have said, "Give me Scotland, or I die."[18] One can make two observations from this statement by Knox. First, John Knox had focus. Whether a person's focus be geographic (i.e., "give me Scotland") or personal (to have the keen awareness of knowing God has placed you in a particular setting), one must embrace the principle of focus when considering the ministry of evangelism. And two, John Knox spoke of sacrifice ("or I die"). Sacrifice is a fundamental and integral ingredient to the ministry of evangelism. I often say to my evangelism students, "If there is one thing I can promise you about the ministry of evangelism it is that this ministry demands a sacrificial servant heart."[19]

Urgency of evangelistic preaching is also noted in the contributions of William Booth, founder of the Salvation Army. From the outset, the reader must know the magnitude of this great servant of the Christian faith. Booth is a clear model of a Christian leader who practiced a sense of urgency in the pulpit. However, Booth's greatest contribution to kingdom advance went far beyond his pulpit ministry. William Booth believed that preaching from the pulpit without practicing a benevolent presence in the marketplace was not a valid expression of Christian ministry.[20] Booth's evangelistic zeal is recorded when speaking at the coronation of King Edward VII: "Your Majesty, some men's ambition is art. Some men's ambition is fame. Some men's ambition is gold. My ambition is the souls of men." It could be said that Booth's financial generosity outside of the pulpit in many ways overshadowed his eloquence in preaching.

Booth's inseparable twofold ministry orientation of evangelistic preaching in the church and acts of selfless charity performed in the community is a

18. Knox scholar Dr. Marcos Seven, writing in the *Genevan Foundation for Cultural Renewal*, cites the famed reformer as saying "Give me Scotland or I die!" (February 15, 2016).

19. Some will take issue with me here, but the ministry of evangelism is one of the harder ministries of the church. This ministry carries with it more than its fair share of rejection. Additionally, it is usually the evangelism or mission budgets in most churches that get sacrificed.

20. One group opposed Booth and the Salvation Army for over a decade because of his involvement with people in great need. They opposed Booth's organized marches against alcohol from the early 1880s until about 1892. Disagreements between the groups resulted in the deaths of several in Booth's organization.

far cry from the steeple-building, media-saturated, personality-driven craze that describes much of "church culture" today. During his lifetime, Booth's ministry was the largest contributor of humanitarian aid in England. Booth's Salvation Army established homes for the homeless, trained the urban poor (including children) in agriculture, made available places of refuge for fallen women, and offered housing and employment to formerly incarcerated prisoners and aid for the poor. Booth and his followers practiced what they preached as they opened up soup kitchens and helped alcoholics get back onto the road to productive living.[21] Additionally, Booth and his Salvation Army did not care if they were ridiculed for their work; they just carried on, because these expressions of ministry were so very necessary. The twin expressions of pulpit ministry and marketplace ministry were inseparable for William Booth, and both were ignited by urgency.

Urgency in Evangelistic Preaching Today

Today's preachers have people sitting before them who are lost in church in the very same way the stay-at-home son in Luke 15 was lost, although he never left home.[22] Truth be told, the younger son had left home long before he physically started his journey into the far country. Those currently in pulpit ministry and those who feel a calling towards preaching as a primary calling on their life must know that people today are searching for something more from life, and more from their preachers! These searchers are coming to church, hoping to have the emptiness and monotony in their lives filled with something of greater substance. During the writing of this chapter, I was a guest preacher in a local church. I held nothing back that morning, though my wife commented, "You could not give that sermon in too many churches." Following the service, a middle aged man's "testimony of depression" was bluntly etched on my heart by his softly spoken words: "Most Sundays when I leave church, I leave more depressed than when I first walked in." In all candor, there were some Sundays as a senior pastor where I was the one in need of encouragement or challenge.

---

21. Today the Salvation Army has adult rehabilitation centers (ARC) all over the United States.

22. I refer to these types of people as "churched, non-Christians." Although these types of people attend a church, they have no personal relationship with Christ. These people often prefer to control their own life rather than have companionship with a loving God.

Our pulpits today must adopt the urgency of Jonathan Edwards and evoke a preaching presence like that of a Richard Baxter, who believed that the sermon he was presently giving might be his last. Or like that of John Knox, whose ministry was geographically focused and driven by unconditional sacrifice. Oh, that our communities across the land would be transformed because pastors delivered sermons with such desperate urgency. And finally, that God would raise up a whole army of Booths for our time; a group of God's ambassadors who would dare to move out from behind the safety of their pulpits and use whatever means necessary to reach others in what might be considered unconventional ways.

Living a life marked by evangelistic urgency begins by having a disciplined mind and a receptive heart that is fully yielded to God. Evangelistic urgency recognizes both small and great needs, and does not hesitate to seize divinely sanctioned opportunities created under the orchestration of the Holy Spirit. Strides of evangelistic urgency breach any gap where previously there has been a chasm of concern found in a hurting world. Evangelistic urgency unashamedly proclaims the good news of Jesus Christ.

Conclusion

Hear now the Father's petition to any heart that is receptive to the call of evangelism:

> Let Me show you the way for all that you today. I will guide you continually so you can relax and enjoy My Presence in the present. Living well is both a discipline and an art. Concentrate on staying close to Me, the divine Artist. Discipline your thoughts to trust Me as I work my ways in your life. Pray about everything; then leave the outcomes up to Me. Do not fear My will, for through it I accomplish what is best for you. Take a deep breath and dive into the depths of absolute trust in Me. Underneath are the everlasting arms![23]

23. Young, *Jesus Calling*, 14.

Questions for Reflection

1. Define urgency. How is this either seen or not seen in your life?

2. From Luke 10, can you identify at least two of the six challenges that hinder evangelistic ministry today?

3. Three principles of evangelistic preaching were identified in a sermon delivered by Jonathan Edwards. What are they?

4. In looking at your own life, would you use the word "urgency" to describe your own interest in the ministry of evangelism?

For Further Reading

Downs, Tim. *Finding Common Ground: How to Communicate With Those Outside the Christian Community . . . While We Still Can.* Chicago: Moody Bible Institute Press, 1999.

Effler, William B. *Turning the Church Inside Out.* N.p.: Worldwide, 2000.

Culpepper, Raymond E. *The Great Commission Connection.* Cleveland: Pathway, 2011.

Hunter, George G. *How To Reach Secular People.* Nashville: Abingdon, 1992.

Kinnaman, David. *You Lost Me.* Grand Rapids: Baker, 2011.

Smith, Sean. *Prophetic Evangelism: Empowering a Generation to Seize Their Day.* Shippensburg, PA: Destiny, 2011.

The Process of Transformation

Lisa Milligan Long, PhD[1]

> Until all of us come to the unity of the faith and of the knowl-
> edge of the Son of God, to maturity, to the measure of the full
> statute of Christ.
>
> —Eph 4:13[2]

Coming to Terms with the Terms

THE TERM "CHRISTIAN SPIRITUALITY" has become quite common in ministry. Yet, it is a term that we sometimes use without thinking about what
it means. We often don't consider what differentiates Christian spirituality
from other forms of spirituality (for example, Hindu spirituality, New Age
spirituality, or Kabbalah spirituality). To truly understand spiritual formation as it relates to ourselves and others in our ministry contexts, we must
first understand the term.

There are numerous definitions of Christian spirituality. One that I
particularly like is as follows: "Christian spirituality is the development

1. Lisa Long serves as an Associate Professor of Christian Formation in the Christian Ministries Department at Lee University. Dr. Long is also the Director of Graduate
Programs in Christian Ministries. She is a graduate of Talbot School of Theology, Biola
University, with a PhD in Religious Education Studies. In addition to her academic work,
Dr. Long has several years of experience in the corporate world and in various ministry
positions in the local church. Her primary areas of research include Christian formation in the Wesleyan Pentecostal tradition and the role of sacramental practices in the
transformation process.

2. All Scripture quotations are from the New Revised Standard Version (NRSV) unless otherwise noted.

of a conscious relationship with God, in Jesus Christ, through the Holy Spirit, within the context of a community of believers that fosters that relationship, as well as the person's understanding of—and response to—that relationship."[3] This is a good definition, but contains quite a few components. Let's break the term down to a more basic level. We understand the word "Christian" to be a designation of the type of spirituality. While "Christian" can be used to indicate Christlike behavior, in this case it is more reflective of something that relates or pertains to Christian doctrine, something that has its origins in the teachings of Christ. The word "spirituality" is a more difficult term to define, particularly because of its current trendiness in postmodern culture. D. A. Carson contends that spirituality is "an ill-defined, amorphous entity that covers all kinds of phenomena," a term that often "functions in the spiritual realm the way 'apple pie' functions in the culinary realm."[4] Nonetheless, we must attempt to clarify what we mean by the word "spirituality."

You might be wondering, "Why the concern with defining the term? After all, does it really matter if the term is somewhat ambiguous?" Yes, it matters! The frequent use of "spirituality" as both a concept and as practice outside the realm of Christianity causes confusion among many immature Christians. Often those whom we are discipling innocently venture into avenues of spirituality that are far outside the bounds of Christian thought and practice. That isn't their intention, but without clarity and sound teaching, how are they to know? It goes without saying that, in order to effectively keep our curious sheep from straying into dangerous territory, we must understand Christian spirituality ourselves.

Carson raises three concerns that result from what might be depicted as fuzzy definitions of Christian spirituality. First, "spirituality is a theological construct,"[5] that is, it is not directly stated in Scripture, but is an idea constructed from theological reflection. Of even more concern is that spirituality is a theological construct without readily agreed-upon essential components (unlike, for example, the doctrine of the Trinity).[6] Of further concern is that the construct, or understanding of spirituality, varies from

---

3. This definition of the term "Christian spirituality" is adapted from the Society for Children's Spirituality's ongoing process of defining the term. Their most recent definition is found at the Society's website: www.childspirituality.org.

4. Carson, "When is Spirituality Spiritual?", 381.

5. Carson, "When is Spirituality Spiritual?", 387.

6. Carson, "When is Spirituality Spiritual?", 387.

person to person. As a result, when one reads about "spirituality," one must try to determine the writer's underlying context.[7] In other words, before we can truly understand someone's approach to spirituality, we need to understand their theological background, their cultural context, and even their personal history.

Additionally, Carson is concerned that multiple or undetermined definitions of Christian spirituality might cause spirituality to "devolve into a technique."[8] And techniques, he claims, are not value-neutral.[9] Insufficient understanding of the theological underpinnings of Christian spirituality make us more willing to accept techniques that may not support our theology, and might even oppose our theology. We must also be aware that techniques are not always transferrable from context to context.[10] Even within a particular faith tradition (e.g., the Church of God), techniques that work in one context might not work in another (e.g., an urban northeastern context to a southwestern rural context). Definitions of Christian spirituality that incorporate either a particular theological tradition or, at the least, recognize the need for a continued conversation between theology and spirituality, will alleviate the devolution into technique that Carson decries.

A final concern raised by Carson is that spirituality is, in many congregations, becoming "the new *summum bonum* [the highest good] by which all things are to be tested."[11] Rather than testing theology or lifestyle by some arbitrary measure of spirituality, spirituality must meet the test of Scripture. It is Scripture that is the *summum bonum* of both Christian theology and Christian practice, and, therefore, of Christian spirituality. Christian spirituality, in both "doctrine" and practice, must be viewed in light of the revelation of God provided in Scripture. The means by which we might better know God must meet the test of Scripture. They may not be clearly denoted in Scripture, but they cannot oppose Scripture. Such an understanding would allow the use of spiritual practices deemed to be both reliable and fruitful throughout the history of church tradition.

Ironically, while Carson denotes several concerns with a lack of definitive understanding of the term "Christian spirituality," he doesn't offer a definition for consideration. He comes close to defining the term when he

7. Carson, "When is Spirituality Spiritual?", 387.

8. Carson, "When is Spirituality Spiritual?", 388.

9. Carson, "When is Spirituality Spiritual?", 388.

10. Carson, "When is Spirituality Spiritual?", 388.

11. Carson, "When is Spirituality Spiritual?", 390.

states that, if what we mean by spirituality is "life-transforming knowledge of God," then we should stress spirituality.[12] This understanding of spirituality as transforming lives is rather common in other attempts to explain the concept.

Alister McGrath offers the following definition of spirituality, one that exemplifies both the transformation resident in Christian spirituality and the totality of that transformation:

> Spirituality is all about the way in which we encounter and experience God, and the transformation of our consciousness and our lives as a result of that encounter and experience. It is most emphatically not the exclusive preserve of some spiritual elite, preoccupied with unhealthy perfectionist tendencies. It is the common duty and joy of all Christian believers, as they long to enter into the deeper fellowship with the living God which is promised in the Scriptures. We can think of it in terms of the *internalization of our faith*. It means allowing our faith to saturate every aspect of our lives, infecting and affecting our thinking, feeling, and living. Nobody can doubt how much we need to deepen the quality of our Christian lives and experience, with God's gracious assistance, and live more authentic lives in which we experience to the full the wonder of the love and grace of God. It is about ways in which we can foster and sustain our personal relationship with Christ. Christian spirituality may be thus understood as the way in which Christian individuals or groups aim to deepen their experience of God.[13]

There is much about this definition that I like. It is helpful to me to think of spirituality as the internalization of our faith. In this sense, faith is not merely something we possess or profess. Rather, it is something that has become an essential part of our very being. In other words, our Christianity could no more be separated from us than could our physical brain or the thoughts within our mind. McGrath also refers to spirituality as saturating our lives. Perhaps you have seen a natural sponge (not the pink or blue ones we buy in the local supermarket). These were living animals whose bodies consisted of pores and channels used to circulate water throughout their bodies—to saturate them with life-sustaining food and oxygen and to move harmful waste out of their bodies. What a powerful image of spirituality!

12. Carson, "When is Spirituality Spiritual?", 392.
13. McGrath, "Loving God with Heart and Mind," para. 9.

Moving from Christian Spirituality to Christian Formation

The process of transformation is at the heart of Christian formation. The idea of formation denotes that something is being shaped or created. At some point, the forming ends, and there is a new creation. It is important to realize that, when referring to our spiritual transformation, the formative process won't end in this life, but will culminate when we are in our glorified (or fully transformed) state in eternity. This understanding leads Les Steele to use the rather awkward term "Christian maturing," rather than "Christian maturity." Maturity, he contends, implies that this is a goal we can attain in this life. Maturing, on the other hand, reminds us that it is a continuing process.[14] *that only God can finish*

How, then, might we define Christian formation? Steele contends that it is the "process of becoming what we were first intended to be and are now allowed to be by the justifying work of Christ."[15] In other words, it is restoring us toward the perfection of created humankind prior to the fall. Christian formation has also been described as the re-formation of the broken soul. Notice the punctuation. It is not the reformation of the broken soul, but the re-formation of what was broken by sin, both original sin and our own personal sin. With this understanding, we next turn our attention to how Christian spiritual formation occurs.

The Process of Transformation

Up to this point, there has been frequent mention of spiritual practices and techniques. You have likely made the connection to the idea that transformation, or Christian formation, isn't solely the work of God in our lives. Steele reminds us that "spiritual formation is the result of God's initiative and our actions."[16] Christian formation is a rather unique partnership between the individual person and the Holy Spirit. It is the Holy Spirit that initiates within us the beginning of transformation. This occurs at the instant we accept God's offer of salvation. When we are "born again," the transformation begins. Unlike *The Curious Case of Benjamin Button* (a movie released in 2008, based on a short story by F. Scott Fitzgerald), a newborn person doesn't emerge from the womb as a fully mature adult; neither are we, in our newborn spirituality, fully mature.

14. Steele, *On The Way*, 11.
15. Steele, *On The Way*, 24.
16. Steele, *On The Way*, 10.

The work of the Holy Spirit doesn't end at our new birth. The so-called *paraclete* passages in John's Gospel (John 14–16) reveal much about the role of the Holy Spirit in our ongoing transformation. While you are likely aware that the *paraclete* (literally, "one called alongside") will serve as counselor, comforter, and advocate (the words most commonly used as English translations of *paraclete*), I wonder if you have given thought to the implications for our spiritual growth. Christ's words promise that the Holy Spirit will teach us of Christ, convict us of sin, and guide us throughout the rest of our journey. Surely you see the connections of those actions and our spiritual transformation!

I have often wondered why God doesn't choose to "zap" us and make us spiritually mature, either at the point of salvation or somewhere along the journey. The answer has much to do with free will and loving obedience as opposed to slavish obedience without choice. We must choose to participate in God's plan of transformation. The means by which we participate are often categorized under the rubric of spiritual disciplines. While there are additional practices that might be included, Richard Foster denotes twelve classic spiritual disciplines:[17]

Inward Disciplines	Meditation
	Prayer
	Fasting
	Study
Outward Disciplines	Simplicity
	Solitude
	Submission
	Service
Corporate Disciplines	Confession
	Worship
	Guidance
	Celebration

Practicing these spiritual disciplines doesn't automatically transform us into spiritual giants. They aren't some sort of magic panacea that cures all our spiritual immaturities. Rather, they allow us to place ourselves before God so that God can transform us. They do this by taking the spotlight off of

17. Foster, *Celebration of Discipline*, v. The list is found in the Table of Contents, and Foster describes and explains the practice of each of these disciplines in the book.

ourselves and centering our focus on God. Faithful and routine practice of the spiritual disciplines equips us to face whatever life offers. Here's a simple example. Think of whatever hobby you love. For me, it is golf. When I first began to play golf, I approached every swing of the club with an intense thought process: how do I hold the club, how do I stand, how do I move the club away from the ball, where should my head be—the list went on and on. Now, after several years of playing golf, I approach a shot much more automatically. It is as though my body "knows" what to do. However, sometimes things get a bit "off" with my game, and shots begin to go awry. That's when I return to the thinking, checking before each shot to make certain I'm doing what I know to do. Slowly but surely, I am being transformed from a hacker to a golfer. The idea is the same with your favorite hobby, and it is also the same with our spiritual transformation. The more we practice (or discipline ourselves) in things that promote spiritual growth, the more the transformation becomes evident and the less we have to think about our spiritual maturing.

Transformed into What?

The notion of transformation or re-formation is wonderful. And while we understand that we won't reach our goal of maturity until glorification, it is helpful to know what Christian maturity might be. In other words, what is the goal of Christian formation? The answer is rather simple. Humankind was created in the image of God, but that image was marred by sin. (Note that the image wasn't eradicated, only marred.) Christian formation is seeking to restore within us a clear reflection of God. In an earlier work, I examined the biblical goal of Christian formation:

> The biblical goal of Christian formation is, quite simply, the full reflection of the image of Christ in the entire life of the follower of Christ. Such an understanding is founded upon Paul's repeated injunctions to Christians to be continually transformed into the image or glory of God (e.g. Rom 8:29, 12:1–2; 1 Cor 15:49; 2 Cor 3:18; Col 3:10) and finds support in a myriad of writings by experts in the field of Christian spiritual formation. Steele (1998) describes Christian formation as the process of returning to the image of God in which humankind was created. Wilkins (1997) argues that "the overarching goal of the entire Christian life" (p. 25) is to become like Christ, to reflect the image of Christ. Dettoni (1994) explains this transformation as Christ being formed within the Christian so they may mature as his disciples. Boa provides further explanation:

"The spiritual life is an all-encompassing, lifelong response to God's gracious initiatives in the lives of those whose trust is centered in the person and work of Jesus Christ. Biblical spirituality is a Christ-centered orientation to every component of life through the mediating power of the indwelling Holy Spirit. It is a journey of the spirit that begins with the gift of forgiveness and life in Christ and progresses through faith and obedience."[18]

To summarize, we are to be transformed into Christlikeness. Excellent! But what does it mean to be Christlike? The best way to answer this question is to reflect on the characteristics of Christ. How would you describe Christ to a friend? Perhaps you would describe Christ as loving, compassionate, just, honest, good, kind, reliable, etc. The list could go on and on. The important thing is that those same characteristics should be evident in our maturing Christian lives. This isn't easy, and it isn't instantaneous. It also isn't optional. In the verses referenced above, the message is clear—transformation into Christlike-ness isn't a choice, but a command. So the obvious connection is that Christian spiritual formation isn't optional. It is an imperative for the individual.

Conclusion

While it is clear that facilitating Christian growth into Christlikeness is an essential aspect of the mission of the church, it is often less clear how such growth might be attained. The lack of clarity begins with a vague and rapidly-changing understanding of the basic terms related to the concept. To better promote Christian growth, we begin by understanding Christian spirituality as related to the ways in which we encounter God, and thus develop our personal relationship with God. This developing relationship is one of transformation—being transformed from one who is alienated from God and bears little or no resemblance to Christ into one who is continually striving to reflect the restored *imago Dei*, the image of God, in day-to-day encounters with God and others. While this work of transformation is initiated by the Holy Spirit, we also bear individual responsibility to engage in practices that turn our attention Godward and develop within our lives what might be termed "holy habits." As leaders in the church, we must be careful to neither neglect our own personal Christian formation nor the formation of those in our care.

18. Long, "Exploratory Study," 51.

Questions for Reflection

1. This chapter provides multiple definitions of the term "Christian spirituality." In your own words, how would you define or describe this term?

2. Sometimes analogies help us understand difficult terms (as in the analogy of a saturated sponge and Christian spirituality). What analogy might you use to help someone understand the concept of transformation into Christlikeness? Make certain you explain the analogy in your response.

3. As you read the categories of Foster's classic spiritual disciplines, toward which category (inward disciplines, outward disciplines, and corporate disciplines) are you most inclined? Why do you think this is so, and what does this reveal to you about your personal approach toward spiritual growth?

4. The church in general is often depicted as not being intentional in assisting Christians in their spiritual growth and transformation toward Christlikeness. Do you agree or disagree with this contention, and why?

For Further Reading

Ford, Marcia. *Traditions of the Ancients: Vintage Faith Practices for the 21st Century.* Nashville: Broadman & Holman, 2006.

Foster, Richard. *Prayer: Finding the Heart's True Home.* New York: HarperSan Francisco, 1992.

Moore, T. M. *Disciplines of Grace: From Spiritual Routines to Spiritual Renewal.* Downers Grove: InterVarsity, 2001.

Wilkins, Michael. *In His Image: Reflecting Christ in Everyday Life.* Colorado Springs: NavPress, 1997.

Willard, Dallas. *Renovation of the Heart: Putting on the Character of Christ.* Colorado Springs: NavPress, 2002.

The Foundation of Discipleship

Bob Bayles, PhD[1]

> Go therefore and make disciples of all the nations, baptiz-
> ing them in the name of the Father and the Son and the Holy
> Spirit, teaching them to observe all that I commanded you; and
> lo, I am with you always, even to the end of the age.
>
> —MATT 28:19–20[2]

IN 1859, CHARLES DICKENS wrote, "It was the best of times, it was the worst
of times."[3] Such could serve as a commentary on the state of discipleship in
the early half of the twenty-first-century American Evangelical church. While
Dickens's work, *A Tale of Two Cities,* was a description of London and Paris in
the late eighteenth century, his words could very well open a narrative on our
contemporary efforts toward a biblical imperative—make disciples!

1. Bob Bayles serves as professor of Discipleship and Christian Formation in the
Christian Ministries Department at Lee University. He holds the Ph.D. degree from Trinity Evangelical Divinity School, Deerfield, Illinois. His background includes 30 years of
local church work at the staff level including children's pastor, youth pastor, Christian
school headmaster, associate pastor and Minister of Education. He has spent more than
20 years teaching in higher education at both the undergraduate and graduate levels,
including international opportunities in China, Korea, Israel, Zambia and Cyprus. He
is the author of a book on local church ministry, and chapter contributions to other
publications and serval articles for church publications. He is married to Terrie and they
have six children, three biological and three adopted from China. He currently serves as
an Elder at his local church.

2. All Scripture quotations are from the New American Standard Bible (NASB) unless otherwise noted.

3. Dickens, *Tale of Two Cities,* 1.

It was the "best of times." In this sense, never before has there been so much opportunity for discipleship. 99.9 percent of Protestant church pastors would no doubt list making disciples as a priority of their congregation. We have more bookstores, publishers, internet sites, curriculum choices, radio, television, and study Bibles than ever before. Never in the history of the Christian church has the remarkable opportunity of the church to disciple its members been available. Surely these are the "best of times."

But in a remarkable dualism, these are also the "worst of times." Research group after research group are identifying critical flaws in many (most?) American church discipleship programs. It is estimated that we are losing anywhere between 70–88 percent of churched youth before the end of their freshman year in college, or age nineteen.[4] More on this in the conclusion. Many/most churches have full-time youth pastors, children's pastors and music pastors, but very few churches have full-time "discipleship pastors." Most operate on a corporate model of a staff person for every age group with little cooperation in the scope and sequence of curriculum for various age groups. To be sure, many are doing a good job, if by that we mean quantitative. The qualitative side of "discipleship" is a little more elusive, again as evidenced by some fairly substantial data.

It is the purpose of this chapter to explore the concept of discipleship from a Biblical perspective. We will look at images in the Old Testament, definitions and patterns in the New Testament, and then examine modern context(s) and opportunities that may be available to us. We will conclude with the state of contemporary discipleship and future trends.

Discipleship

The very simplest definition of a disciple is one who learns from a master teacher and follows that master teacher's lifestyle and teachings. This would be true for most religions, but especially Christianity. The word *mathetes* (μαθητής), or disciple, is used more than 250 times in the New Testament to identify the followers of Christ, most often of his immediate group we identify as the Twelve. But certainly this term has broader implications to include anyone claiming allegiance to Christ. We will take a more in-depth look at this word as it is used in the Bible.

4. Smith and Denton, *Soul Searching*; Barna Group, "Six Reasons," https://www.barna.com/research/six-reasons-young-christians-leave-church/; Kosmin, "New Survey," http://commons.trincoll.edu/aris/files/2013/11/ARIS-Student-Survey-Press-Release-2013.pdf

Old Testament

Discipleship, defined as a teacher/pupil relationship, is not explicitly present in the Old Testament. There are examples and patterns of teaching and learning, but the idea of a master teacher gathering pupils to their side for the purpose of instruction is largely absent from the Old Testament.[5] What is present are culturally embedded processes.

Deuteronomy 6 is often lifted up as the "Queen" of Old Testament passages dealing with education. Moses is dying and he is again giving the nation of Israel a summary of his teachings. In 6:4–25, Moses states that parents are to "teach" their children. The idea here carries with it the continuing sharpening of a knife blade. "Teach your children" is not a one-time act. The tense of the verb indicates ongoing, continual action. While specifically directed to the parents, the entire nation of Israel was ultimately responsible for this teaching. So, in Deuteronomy 6, the parents were the primary disciplers of their children.

First Kings initiates the story of Elijah and Elisha. As their relationship unfolds in subsequent chapters, it appears that there is a "mentoring" relationship at work.[6] Elijah appears to be the wise old sage/prophet who has seen his ups and downs. He is the "mentor" to the younger Elisha. When Elijah gets taken into heaven, Elisha becomes his replacement on Earth.

There are multiple references in 1 Samuel and 2 Kings to something called "the schools of the prophets." We are not entirely sure what this meant, but in the least is the referral of some type of education and/or training. These were bans of men who learned from the older, wiser prophets.

The Proverbs and Psalms (wisdom literature) are filled with examples of learning, teaching, obeying, and following the law of the Lord. There are a variety of ways this is done in the wisdom literature materials, but the end result is that the people of God would be faithful to the words of the Lord, to his law and teachings.

---

5. For a good brief read of "discipleship" in the Old Testament, see Hull, *Complete Book of Discipleship*, 52–58.

6. Mentoring is a twentieth-century word, rooted in imagery in a variety of settings. I am using "mentoring" as it is well-known by the reader and helps explain "discipleship," though there are differences between the two terms.

New Testament

The scene changes entirely as we enter the New Testament world. The roughly four hundred years between the Testaments has produced startling changes in the educational world of the New Testament. It is a world profoundly influenced by Greek thought.[7] Also, fully embedded in the Greek world was the master-teacher/philosopher and his students.

The Gospels are replete with examples of disciples and discipleship. In fact, we only see use of *mathetes* (μαθητή), or disciple, in the four gospels and the book of Acts. Paul does not use this specific word anywhere in his epistles. So, for the writers of the four gospels, the choice of "disciple" is a specific and intention term used to convey something very precise about the nature of what Jesus was doing with people, particularly the Twelve.

There are areas of similarity between the Greek scholar and their student(s), and Jesus and the Twelve. In both, we find a master teacher conveying a body of truths to his followers, students, pupils or learners. These four words are synonymous in the ancient understanding of a disciple. The student's role was to voluntarily attach himself/herself to the master teacher for the purposes of acquiring certain truths.

However, there are important differences in the manner and approach of Jesus in selecting the Twelve to be his followers. First, a Greek scholar would never have actually sought out students. Students came to the scholar. With Jesus, he actively sought his disciples, personally going after them and calling them by name (see Mark 3). Second, the goal of Greek philosophy student was to one day become the master teacher, the scholar. However, with Jesus' call comes the perpetual call to be a follower, a student, a disciple, never to be the Rabbi/scholar. Never is it inherent to the call of Christ for one to become above another. There are no ranks or degrees of disciple in the New Testament. Such delineations would lead to arrogance, which Christ taught specifically against. Later, Paul will reference this with statements like "the preaching of the cross is foolishness to those who do not believe"; "I count all things loss except for a knowledge of Jesus Christ."

Jesus' use of disciple is enlightening. It is in his words that we find primary purpose to what it means to be a disciple. First, Luke 9:57–62 gives us Jesus' description of three different types of people who desire to be a follower,

7. We have in mind here Socrates, Plato, and Aristotle primarily. However the influence of these men can also be seen in what is known as the "Socratic method," or question/answer. Jesus was masterful in this methodology of teaching.

yet are making lethal mistakes about the nature of discipleship. Dietrich Bonhoeffer gives an excellent exegesis of this passage, and the following are representative of his thoughts:[8] Do you see yourself in any of these men?

Disciple #1: Note how this man initiates the call to follow Jesus. He does not wait for Jesus to call him. Jesus warns him that he does not know what he is doing, and that the call of discipleship cannot be self-initiated.

Disciple #2: Jesus does issue the call to this man, but the man wishes to first bury his father—a noble task to be sure. But nothing (in this case the law) can trump the call of Christ to follow him.

Disciple #3: Again, this man initiates the call, but what is different from the first man is that this man stipulates his own terms for following Christ.

Mark 3 is perhaps one of the most insightful passages on "calling" to be a disciple.[9] However, if the reader is too quick to read, they will gloss right over one of the most powerful pieces of the calling of the Twelve. In this passage, Jesus goes up to a mountain and calls the twelve that he would have follow him, sending them out to preach the gospel and cast out demons. But something is missing. Mark (with most probably Peter as his source) states that Jesus first wanted to spend time with the disciples. Translation: we cannot/should not preach the gospel or attempt to cast out demons (or any other ministerial activity) without first spending time with Christ. And this is the part that a quick read of Mark will miss: spending time with Christ is essential to ministerial effectiveness. All the "stuff" Jesus calls us to do will simply be just that without the personal relationship coming first. It is imperative that you not miss this point. You cannot claim to be a disciple of Christ and not spend time with him.

A last critical passage cannot be overlooked, Matthew 28:16–20, frequently known as the "Great Commission." The newly resurrected Christ gathers his followers on a mountain, they worship him, and then Jesus states, "Go therefore and make disciples of all the nations, baptizing them in the name of the Father and the Son and the Holy Spirit, teaching them to observe all that I commanded you; and lo, I am with you always, even to the end of the age." Here is a quick Greek lesson: verbs are critical to understanding the action being done in a sentence. In this passage, four verbs exist: go, make disciples, baptize, and teach. However, there is only one leading verb, the

---

8. Bonhoeffer, *Cost of Discipleship*, 60–63.

9. I am personally indebted to Dr. Terry Cross, Dean of the School of Religion, for these thoughts. He has lectured for me in the mission of the church for five years, and I first heard this understanding of Mark 3 from him.

imperative verb, in the Great Commission. It is the verb meaning to "make disciples." "Go," "teach," and "baptize" are participles which, in this case, lend support to the imperative, or the command verb. In other words, the making of disciples is the most important of the four verbs. As important as evangelism, teaching, and water baptism are, they all find their truest meaning in the making of disciples. Do not misunderstand—the verbs are not in competition with one another. The three verbs complement the lead verb: "make disciples." It is that verb that Christ elevates to the command level—we simply have no choice but to make disciples.

The Book of Acts

The book of Acts continues this discipleship theme, particularly the last words of Jesus in Matthew's gospel. One of the central themes of Acts is to trace how the disciples spread the gospel to "all the world." As most readers of the New Testament will know, the book of Acts is a central book in that two primary points are made. First, the gospel is for all people, not just the Jewish people (Acts 1:8; 10; 15). Second, the book of Acts records the conversion of Saul (Acts 9), and is one of the most important chapters in the Bible (ranking in importance to Genesis 12 and the call of Abraham, and Exodus 3 and the call of Moses). With the Apostle Paul, we see a huge shift from the church being primarily a Jewish entity to primarily a gentile entity, though Paul warns us in Ephesians 2 about the wall that can so easily divide us.

It seems one of the more subtle shifts in Acts is the association of teaching by the disciples with the new community developing. Acts 2:42–47 is a potent passage on discipleship and community. They studied together, ate together, broke bread together (a possible reference to communion), worshiped together, and evangelized together. From my reading of this passage, it seems that discipleship and community cannot be divorced and still be healthy. I also believe this is the reason for two of Bonhoeffer's most loved books, *The Cost of Discipleship* and *Life Together*—both highly recommended reads. As noted by former Lee University professor Dr. John Sims, the first act of the newly Spirit-filled church was the study of the apostles' doctrine.[10] Interestingly enough, it was not the demonstration of a spiritual gift(s)—though these are vitally important to the New Testament church—but the study of God's word that is first mentioned by Luke in 2:42. Sims goes on to state, "From a New Testament perspective, learning and

10. Sims, *Our Pentecostal Heritage*, 42.

education can never be rightly divorced from true spirituality."[11] I would like to take the liberty to modify this by stating from a biblical perspective that learning and education can never be rightly divorced from what it means to be a disciple, a follower of Christ.

Paul

Perhaps no man (other than Jesus himself) has had more influence on the world than the Apostle Paul. Listen to his own words describing himself: "I myself might have confidence even in the flesh. If anyone else has a mind to put confidence in the flesh, I far more: circumcised the eighth day, of the nation of Israel, of the tribe of Benjamin, a Hebrew of Hebrews; as to the Law, a Pharisee; as to zeal, a persecutor of the church; as to the righteousness which is in the Law, found blameless" (Phil 3:4–7). Paul was rabbi, scholar, teacher, student, Pharisee—unquestionably the most educated of the first-century church leaders. So with all his understanding of learning, teaching, and the Jewish rabbi/student relationship, why did Paul apparently choose to not use *mathetes*, the word most associated with the term "disciple"? It would have been a word instantly recognized by most of his converts, gentiles steeped in the Greek tradition spoken of earlier. Rather, Paul primarily chooses another Greek word, *mimeomai* (μιμέομαι), from which we get the English word "mimic," meaning "to copy." Listen to his words in 1 Corinthians 11:1: "Be imitators of me, just as I also am of Christ." Over and again, Paul uses this phrase to characterize his understanding of what it means to be a follower of Christ. There is a fixed standard or pattern that we must emulate. Obviously, that pattern is found in Scripture, but Paul's point was clearly that he was emulating that pattern. To follow Paul (not in some narcissistic meaning, but in true humility) was the same as following the patterns outlined in Scripture. The compelling question behind this phrase, for twenty-first-century Christians, is can we say to others "follow me and you will be following Christ" as forcefully as Paul stated it two thousand years ago? Are our lives so intimately patterned after Scripture that someone could follow us without using the Bible and be following Christ? Sobering question.

---

11. Sims, *Our Pentecostal Heritage*, 42.

The Modern Church—Evangelical America in the First Half of the Twenty-First Century

Our attention now shifts in this last section of this chapter to where we are in the contemporary church, and trends that appear to be on the horizon. Referring back to the third footnote, there are multiple, unrelated sources stating that the condition of many churches in the arena of discipleship is dismal at best. How is it, with all the information, technology, and resources at our disposal, that the church is doing such a mediocre (at best) job in the area of discipleship? This is assuming, of course, that the resources listed in footnote three are accurate. If we take seriously Matthew 28:19–20, and the imperative (command, not suggestion) verb meaning to "make disciples," we should be very concerned. It is very easy at this juncture to get negative: the church is not doing this, the church is not doing that. Allow me, rather, to propose to you some thoughts in summary form of what the church might refocus on.

Trend 1: I believe one of the areas the church has attempted to re-cover is the formation and/or strengthening of the small group movement so powerful in the 1980s and 1990s. Given the fact that the average-sized Protestant church in America is seventy-five (not ten thousand), many churches are already using a "small group" paradigm; they just might not define it as such. Smaller churches tend to be more community-centered by default, if not by design. At a church of seventy-five, everybody knows everybody's name anyway. But in larger churches, you can get lost; you can become a spectator that slips in and out of a service unnoticed. This is the reason many larger churches depend so very much on small groups. They are places where people connect and "discipleship" happens—at least in theory. So one step in the right direction is the small-group movement, as long as these small groups are correctly organized and maintained.

Trend 2: I believe that another positive movement forward is the shift from viewing discipleship as a program to discipleship as a process. Americans have been groomed on the idea/philosophy of ten quick steps to cure all our ails. The church is not immune from this either, obviously. We have been trained to think that Sunday School is sufficient theological education for our children, youth, and adults. One hour a week provides a biblical/theological foundation for life. We have been trained to think, "if I go to small groups 70% of the time, I will get all the community and in-depth Bible study I need for the week." And the pattern emerges in many (most) of our church programming. Proof test: ask 98 percent of pastors to describe their church, and they will begin with listing the programs rather than talking about the people that they serve. It is just in our nature. It is not that programs are bad, but programs alone must not define discipleship. Attend a certain number of meetings, go to this number of Bible studies, and you will be a disciple. However, discipleship is a lifelong process. We never "arrive" at being fully complete until death.

Trend 3: Finally, I believe another, somewhat-overlooked element of discipleship is the incalculable value of the home in the process. There is not space here to identify all the theologians in church history that continually warn the church that parents must be a vital part of the theological training of their children.[12] We do encounter problems with this when parents themselves are not adequately trained, and so the argument has now come full circle. Discipleship is about education—biblical, theological, church history, and so on. When parents are equipped properly, the discipleship process flows more naturally and effectively. Teaching/discipleship done in the home becomes a natural part of what the child lives out and sees happening at the church. There is a holism to their theological education, not fragmentation.

The mandate from Christ is clear: discipleship is not optional. We must provide training and education to the next generation. It is a process. It frequently involves small groups. It must involve the home/parents.

Conclusion

Discipleship is a difficult area to define if using empirical data as the proof. It is much more nuanced than simply saying "we discipled thirty people this past year at our church." Discipleship is defined in many ways by many different movements and people. The Old Testament gives us a peek into this process, and while not fully defining it as clearly as the New Testament, stories like Eli and Samuel, Elijah and Elisha, and the school of the prophets helps us to understand that this was a mentoring element to Old Testament interpersonal relationships. The New Testament is quite clear on the purposes of discipleship. Matthew 28 is very often the go-to passage

---

12. Having done extensive work on this in other non-published materials, suffice it to say that Martin Luther, John Calvin, Richard Baxter, and John Wesley wrote prophetically about the role of the parent in theological education and the dire consequences of what happens when it is not done. These four church fathers describe the consequences on society and the church when children are left bereft of biblical/theological training.

for discipleship, and we learned there that discipleship is in the imperative tense in the Greek. There simply is no choice but that we do discipleship. How we do it may vary; that we do it is not in question. Paul goes on to give us the metaphor of "mimicking" or "imitating" as his primary model of discipleship. There is a lot of work yet to be done on these powerful words defining discipleship. We have ended our discussion with three trends. There are more, but these are (in my opinion) defining trends which cannot be ignored.

It is hoped that you have read this chapter closely and walk away from it with a renewed sense of urgency in the body of Christ for true, biblical discipleship. It is imperative. After all, we call it the Great Commission, not the Great Suggestion.

Questions for Reflection

1. How and to what extent are the Old and New Testaments similar (and dissimilar) in the discussion of discipleship?

2. It was stated in the chapter that study of the apostles' doctrine was a first major act of the newly empowered Christian church (Acts 2). What connection(s) is there between discipleship and study/learning? Why is this so very important for our contemporary setting?

3. What major contribution(s) does Paul add to our understanding of discipleship, and why is this important?

4. Of the three trends listed, which resonates with you the most? Why? What implications are there for your ministry?

For Further Reading

Baxter, Richard. *The Reformed Pastor*. Richmond: John Knox, 1956.

Bayles, Bob, and Timothy K. Beougher. "Richard Baxter: Educating Through Pastoral Discipleship," In *A Legacy of Religious Educators: Historical and Theological Introductions*. Lynchburg, VA: Liberty University, 2017.

Bonhoeffer, Dietrich. *The Cost of Discipleship*. New York: Simon & Schuster, 1959.

Hull, Bill. *The Complete Book of Discipleship*. Colorado Springs: NavPress, 2006.

The Heart of Worship

Jerald J. Daffe, DMin[1]

Amen!
Praise and glory
And wisdom and thanks
and honor and power and strength
be to our God for ever and ever.
Amen!

—Rev 7:12[2]

ONE WOMAN SITS SILENTLY with eyes closed and head bowed. Another one joyously expresses verbal praise with exclamations of "hallelujah" and "praise the Lord."

Which of these two women is offering genuine worship?

One congregation follows a tightly scripted pattern of unison words and postures. Another plans, but moves with the free flow of the Holy Spirit.

Which of these two congregations is offering genuine worship?

---

1. Jerald Daffe is Professor of Pastoral Studies and Coordinator of the pastoral major. He holds a Doctor of Ministry degree, with an emphasis in worship, from Western Conservative Baptist Seminary. His ministry includes ten years of pastoring in North Dakota, fourteen years of teaching at Northwest Bible College, and being on the faculty of Lee University since 1987. Daffe is the author/ co-author of ten books, over seventy articles, and a number of booklets and independent study manuals. His most recent books are *Clothing a Naked Church* and *Crosses, Coffee, Couches, and Community* (an overview of the emergent church movement). He and his wife, Phyllis, have one married daughter.

2. All Scripture quotations are from the New International Version (NIV) unless otherwise noted.

One group sings from the hymnbook accompanied with a piano and organ. Another group sings new praise songs with a band utilizing a wide variety of instruments.

Again the previous question must be asked: which group is offering genuine worship?

More than likely, some individuals reading these varied scenarios immediately want more information. That is a normal request. However for the purpose of this introduction to worship, answer each of these questions within their limited descriptions.

Impacting Factors

It's usually easy to state what we think or believe, but much more difficult to indicate why. Opinions normally do not just arise out of thin air. They tend to be based on one or more impacting factors. Let's consider several of these in relationship to worship and the answers to the previous scenarios.

At the head of the list is the impact of personal preference. Each of us has distinct likes and dislikes, which tend to dominate the major areas of our life. It is no different when considering worship. Certain styles or actions fit more closely to our personality and individual comfort zones. Key events as we go through the seasons of life may influence us to move to a totally different style, or at least to a modified form of our initial preference.

A second influencing factor is personal experience. For many of us, this begins with the style of worship in which we were raised, or the style of worship of the church or group when becoming a believer. This could be either a positive or negative factor, depending upon the total experience. One dimension begins with an individual's spiritual relationship with the Lord Jesus Christ. The more we cherish our relationship with him, the greater should be our desire to worship to the fullest of our ability. Another dimension of personal experience is dependent upon how broad our exposure to a diverse variety of worship styles and settings. This expands one's ability to perceive the breadth of genuine heart-originating worship.

A third factor influencing our perspective of worship is personal knowledge. This moves beyond information gained by experience. It comes from biblical study on the subject of worship and expanding our concepts by reading books and selected articles on the topic. In reference to the biblical study, it is amazing how many people refer only to the Psalms and totally overlook or even avoid all the passages in other books, such as the verse from Revelation shared at the beginning of the chapter.

Working Definition

It is very difficult, and maybe impossible, to get to the heart of worship without having a working definition as our guide. Ask a group of individuals to share their definitions, and you may find a great amount of variance. Unbelievers are more likely to define worship in terms of actions. We refer to this as "hand, knee, and mouth." Believers tend to respond with descriptions of style, emotion, and lifestyle. Most of them are very good, even though usually limited in light of the totality which worship encompasses.

There are many excellent definitions to be found in the multitude of worship books on library and bookstore shelves. Some are a paragraph in length, and others move to the opposite side and are a succinct sentence. Believing that brevity with completeness is a virtue, consider the following one sentence definition. "Worship is our response to God declaring His worth as He has revealed Himself to us."[3]

Our—As human beings, the highest of God's creation, we alone have the capacity, opportunity, and obligations to worship.

Response—We are the doers in this action, not the onlookers. There is to be total participation—physical, emotional, and spiritual. It isn't a compartmentalized activity. Worship is to be reflected in our thoughts, our speaking, and our actions. "Worship is most effective when it connects with the heart (emotions), the mind (intellect), and the body of worshipers as a whole."[4]

To God—Genuine worship has a defined direction. God is the receiver. We are responding to him and the leading of the Holy Spirit, rather than the instructions of a worship leader, no matter how spiritual he or she may be!

Declaring—Worship involves more than a casual suggestion about the God we serve. Genuine worship is an authoritative proclamation about the members of the Trinity. It assumes a personal, knowledgeable, harmonious relationship.

His worth—This is the crucial point. Our worship is to center on God's glory, power, and righteousness. No emphasis should be placed on our value, stature, accomplishments, or actions.

3. Daffe, "Introduction to Worship," 7–8.
4. Boone, "Worship and the Torah," 23.

As he has revealed himself to us—Worship necessitates our having knowledge of God. Because of finite human-ness, we could not come to know him more, but for his self-revelation. This comes through a number of avenues such as Scripture, creation, Jesus Christ, the Holy Spirit, prophetic fulfillment, and specific events in our personal lives.

A working definition for worship provides not only a foundation for understanding, but also for realizing what must be evident if we are engaging in worship which is acceptable to our Heavenly Father. Here is a good place to be reminded that the heart of worship is more involved than simply going to church or fellowship and participating in a preferred set of actions and words.

Before leaving the definition of worship, consideration needs to be given to Romans 12:1: "Therefore, I urge you, brothers and sisters, in view of God's mercy, to offer your bodies as living sacrifices, holy and pleasing to God—this is your true and proper worship."

This passage of Scripture provides a broadened spectrum of what it means to respond in worship. It removes any concept of worship being limited to specifically designated areas or events. Church services, small groups, and personal devotions are only a small segment of what it means to worship.

Since we live in these physical bodies, worship is expanded to all of who we are and what we do on a daily basis, all the time. It entails out motives, attitudes, and actions. We are forced to ask whether or not our treatment of a particular person is consistent with a worshipful action to God. More than likely, if this were kept in the forefront of our thinking, there would be modifications in our interaction with both believers and unbelievers.

A special caution and an emphasis needs to be inserted here. Just being a born-again believer doesn't automatically validate all our actions as worship! The Romans passage in context indicates a conscious giving of an offering.[5] Giving in and of itself doesn't guarantee worship. Once again, it is vital for us to consider the reason for our offering. Deeds stimulated by duty are no different than simply going through the motions. They do not qualify as worship! Unless we serve with gladness of heart, instead of with drudgery or out of habit, then there is no worship.

Genuine God-honoring worship involves intentionality and deliberateness, regardless of when or where it takes place. It "includes the ambitions, thoughts, and intentions of the heart."[6]

5. Adewaya. *Holiness in the Letters of Paul*, 37.
6. Towns and Whaley, *Worship through the Ages*, 57.

Biblical Perspective

Nowhere in Scripture is a particular style outlined and then projected as the pattern for all believers to utilize in their worship. This allows for the inclusion of cultural and personal preferences, which span the centuries. However, Scripture does provide specific directives and examples of worship which enable us to develop principles to guide believers as we participate in a wide variety of styles and forms.

Repeatedly, we are called to give glory and exalt the God of our salvation, as well as bow in worship (Psalm 29:1–2; 99:5–6). Also, there are many calls to offer praise, thanksgiving, and joy. Of specific interest for all of us should be the many examples of worship. The most complete one, in my opinion, is too often hidden or lost in the narrative of the Christmas story.

Let's look at the visit of the Magi, as recorded in Matthew 2. Their desire to worship the newborn King of the Jews stimulates them to put forth the effort of traveling some distance to a foreign country (v. 1). They go to the logical place where the newborn King would be: Jerusalem (v. 1). They rejoice in the confirmation of the star's appearance over Bethlehem (v. 10). Once in the house where the child (Jesus) is, they bow in the presence of divine royalty (v. 11). Then they present appropriate gifts: gold, frankincense, and myrrh (v. 11). Upon receiving a directive from the Lord, they return home by another route (v. 12).

The practical applications for our worship are evident. Four stand out. First, worship develops in an atmosphere of personal effort. Second, worship includes both rejoicing and humble reverence in the presence of God. Third, worship involves our giving of personal resources and giftedness. Fourth, worship brings change, which causes us to leave differently than when we arrived.

Other New Testament accounts provide snapshots of worship as the normal response to divine intervention. After the feeding of the five thousand, the disciples find their boat tossed on the stormy Sea of Galilee. Christ's walking on the water and Peter's subsequent coming to him sets the stage for both worship and a dramatic statement of faith. Jesus saves Peter from sinking in the water and calms the wind. "Then those who were in the boat came and worshiped Him saying, 'Truly You are the Son of God'" (Matt 14:33, NKJV).

Another snapshot is found in the Gospel of John, in the narrative of the healing of the blind man. After receiving his sight, this man inadvertently becomes embroiled in the Pharisee's attempt to discredit Jesus. But in the process, once he expresses his belief that Jesus is the Son of God, he immediately worships (John 9:38).

Then, not to be forgotten are the two post-resurrection appearances recorded in Matthew 28:9 and 17. The Christ who had been crucified and buried is now risen. As the women leave the empty tomb to announce the vacancy to the disciples, Jesus meets them. In his directive to "'Rejoice!' . . . they came and held Him by the feet and worshiped Him" (v. 9, NKJV). Later, when Jesus appears to eleven of the disciples in Galilee, they respond in worship (v. 17).

In all of these examples, worship did not occur because someone was directing or demanding their response. Instead, this was worship which originated from the heart, based on an encounter and relationship. The practical contemporary application for each of us should be quite evident. Our worship should flow from within as the logical result of our relationship with the Lord Jesus Christ and witness to the marvelous works he continues to do in our lives and the lives of other believers! Failure to worship seems to be evidence of spiritual blindness and decay.

Let's consider one more example of worship, as presented in Genesis 4:3–7. The first record of human encounter with God after the expulsion of Adam and Eve from the garden in Eden involves the action of worship. The two brothers, Cain and Abel, each bring their worship offering to the Lord. However, only one is declared acceptable. Because God is just, we must assume that they had been informed of the principles for proper worship in the sight of God. Cain's failure and subsequent anger at God indicates an attitude problem which stems from within.

Heart Issues

The working definition of worship presented earlier uses the term response. It is so easy to immediately think of the exterior physical actions. However, that overlooks the inner spiritual dimension which God requires of our worship. This is readily seen in two passages from the Old Testament: Isaiah 1 and Amos 5. For better understanding, consider reading these two chapters prior to continuing to the rest of this section.

In the first ten verses of Isaiah 1, the prophetic words of the Lord describe a rebellious nation. Using human analogy, their spiritual condition is described as being completely injured and diseased from head to foot. It appears terminal. Plus, there has been no attempt to bring healing by cleansing, medicating or bandaging their wounds and sores. Verse 5 points out the source of their problem. It stems not only from their thinking, but also from their inner loyalty and commitment. Notice how they are compared to Sodom and Gomorrah, the cities God chose to destroy, sparing only Lot, his wife, and two daughters (Gen 19).

Beginning in verse 11, there is a listing of worship actions in which these spiritually deficient people continue to participate. They appear at the temple with offerings. There is the regular celebration of the required feasts commemorating events of their history. God declares that all of their offerings and assemblies are meaningless. He will not listen or respond to their prayers and uplifted hands. It would be far better for them to stop everything than to continue this spiritual affront to a God who knows the real them.

Later in Isaiah, we read the Lord's description of their worship (29:13, NIV). "These people come near to me with their mouth and honor me with their lips, but their hearts are far from me. Their worship of me is based on merely human rules they have been taught."

The same environment is found in Amos's prophetic words to the northern kingdom of Israel (Amos 5:21–23). This is in the same time period of Isaiah's prophecy. These people are also actively involved in actions of worship. They too gather for the festivals. They even bring choice various offerings (some of the best). They sing and play musical instruments. But, with strong words, the Lord indicates that not only will he not listen or accept these activities, he hates them. Once again, it would be far better not to be doing anything than to continue this hypocritical charade.

Consider the actions described by these two prophets as fitting the category of treason. The same could be said of individuals and whole congregations: "Our worship may be an act of treason when we go through all the actions and say all the words but never make that 'connect' with the God we are proclaiming."[7]

A disconnect continues when we believe worship takes place, even when there is unconfessed sins in our lives. The celebration of worship which God accepts cannot take place without the cleansing from sin, which begins with our confession and repentance.

Not to be overlooked is the fact that worship isn't about us and our preferred style. It's all about him!

---

7. Daffe, *Clothing a Naked Church*, 112.

In the New Testament, we find a similar situation with the Pharisees, a religious sect of Judaism. Their undergirding principle was to keep the Law of Moses. They desired to be separated from those who were careless about religious practices. Regretfully, this drive for holiness and separation caused them to develop human traditions in an attempt to keep the law. This produced an external religion, which resulted in scathing rebukes from both John the Baptist and Jesus.

Their self-righteousness became evident in taking pride in public prayers, tithing on the least amount of income, and even wearing a distinguishing garb. They were so concerned about the least items of importance that they totally neglected the most important principles and directives. Matthew 23 records Jesus repeatedly labeling them as hypocrites for failing to practice what they preached to others, and their inside not being what they projected on the outside. He realistically refers to them as blind guides and whitewashed tombs. It is very strong language to describe individuals as a ball of snakes and a tomb of decaying flesh and bones!

The reality which continually appears in all these scenarios is the need for worship from the heart, our inner being, if it is going to be acceptable to God. Actions and words which do not reflect the true condition of one's heart are nothing more than ritual and ceremony, which is despicable in God's sight.

Heavenly Worship

What will it be like to be in heaven? On occasion, one may hear an individual speak of cooling his feet in the crystal river or walking on streets of gold. Others speak of banqueting or facetiously eating all the chocolate they want. Frequently people speak of meeting the saints of old and plying them with questions. A great many speak of meeting their Savior and Lord face-to-face. Shouldn't that be the most desired experience and reason for being in heaven?

One dimension of heaven which may be overlooked is the actions and attitudes of worship. When reading and studying the book of Revelation, it is so easy to become absorbed in the messages to the seven churches and the end-time events that the aspect of worship is missed. There are four glimpses into the activity of heavenly worship. In each, the individuals fall down in the presence of God and worship (Rev 4:10; 5:14; 7:11; 11:16). There are marvelous words of worship which we can and should offer in both our private and public worship. Many of you will recognize them as being portions of the songs we sing.

> Holy, holy, holy is the Lord God Almighty, who was, and is, and is to come. (4:8)

> Worthy is the Lamb who was slain, to receive power and wealth and wisdom and strength and honor and glory and praise. (5:12)

> To him who sits on the throne and to the Lamb be praise and honor and glory and power, for ever and ever. (5:13)

> Salvation belongs to our God, who sits on the throne, and to the Lamb. (7:10)

> We give thanks to you, Lord God Almighty, the one who is and who was. (11:17)

It seems only appropriate that the adoration and glory ascribed in heaven should also be evident in our worship here on Earth. Here again we return to the concept of worship being a heart response. Neglect of our spiritual vitality will keep us from expressing the reverent, joyful worship which spontaneously springs from our inner depths. In contrast, the worship which flows without restriction from a heart of love for God is not only acceptable, but positively impacts all dimensions of one's life.

Earthly Worship

Here is where we get to the nuts and bolts of the topic. In other words, it's time to take a close introspection of our personal worship in both private and corporate settings. It is relatively easy to talk about the biblical and philosophical principles of worship. The real challenge comes when it is time to turn the spotlight on us and our brothers and sisters in Christ.

Are our actions, words, and attitudes genuine heartfelt worship? Or are they patterned responses which stem from habit and the directives of others?

In a beginning psychology class, we are introduced to an interesting experiment conducted by Ivan Pavlov, a Russian physiologist. He would ring a bell and then give food to a dog. After a series of repetitions, he would ring the bell, and the dog would salivate, even though no food was presented. It was a conditioned reflex.

Now let's relate this to our worship. Could it be that our worship is a conditioned response to outside stimuli, rather than stemming from within due to our close relationship with the Lord Jesus Christ? For example, do we lift our hands, say "amen," or clap our hands because the leader tells us to respond in that manner? Or do we react in some form of posture and gesture due to the style of music?

Worship leaders have a definite part in our corporate response, but they are to be the prompters, helping us find our way by suggesting or demonstrating, rather than demanding our actions and words. Music is the greatest art form, enabling us to feel and express our emotions. However, it should be the means for our expression, rather than the source of our worship emotion.

[The key to genuine heartfelt worship lies within each of us on an individual basis. It is the response of a person's total personality—our mind, our emotions, and our will. The mind thinks and meditates on the knowledge of] God and our relationship with Jesus Christ. This information translates into emotions and their related desires. Through each of these steps, the action of the will operates. It either allows or disallows the continuance of worship.

When we have experienced this process on an individual basis, then it automatically becomes evident when we gather as a body of believers to exalt our God. It's difficult to expect people to worship as a corporate body when they haven't worshiped as an individual in private.

Some Reminders

First, not everyone worships in the same posture and gesture. This necessitates our being very careful not to criticize someone's worship simply because it is different from ours. A friend of mine once said, "when we [his denomination] get really happy we look up to heaven and smile." An exaggeration? Yes! But we need to glean the principle of difference from it.

Second, though we may not realize it, we must consider the possibility of being stalemated in our own expressions of posture and gesture. We may need to vary them so the true inner response of worship flows, rather than what we always do at a certain time. Quiet meditation instead of verbal statements may be substituted on occasions. For others, it may mean being far more outgoing in gesture or verbal expressions.

Third, true worship must be in the spirit. This means that it is to be spiritual communication and through the ministry of the Holy Spirit. All of our intellectual and physical activities are of little value, unless they are accompanied by the spiritual dimension of our being.

Fourth, when patterns and forms of worship are practiced without the accompanying heart response to God it is nothing more than pseudo-worship or empty actions, no different than those practiced by heathen or pagan rituals. Sounds very strong! Absolutely. Can it be anything other than that?

Fifth, repeatedly in Scripture we are taught that worship should be in the atmosphere of holiness (1 Chron 16:29; Ps 29:2; 96:9). Approaching God with a deep awareness of his righteousness and holiness brings a new awareness of what it means to have the life of a believer. He is worthy, and we are so unworthy. However, through the regeneration of salvation, we can approach him and be acceptable in his sight!

Conclusion

Worship is at the heart of our relationship with God, our Heavenly Father. Recognizing its importance doesn't automatically produce the desired actions. Personal preference and secular influences combined with a lack of biblical knowledge can contribute to an anemic form of worship with little or no spiritual value. Individual believers and worship leaders are susceptible to these factors, unless there is careful consideration of what comprises genuine worship.

It is so easy to fall prey to the desire to have worship be aesthetically pleasing and emotionally inspiring. This isn't incorrect, as long as the aspects of being biblically enlightening, spiritually discipling, and intellectually stimulating are also integrated.

May we strive to demonstrate the heart of worship in all we do and say to the honor and glory of our God!

Questions for Reflection

1. Why is worship so important to a believer's spiritual being?

2. What are some ways in which worship may contribute to spiritual growth or transformation?

3. How is it possible that our desire for excellence in our corporate worship settings may cross over into the category of entertainment?

4. Suggest some ways to help individuals expand their understanding and appreciation for worship styles other than their own.

5. What are some questions all believers should ask themselves as part of evaluating their worship?

6. In light of the conclusion, which factors are dominant in your personal preference of worship style?

For Further Reading

Benson, Bruce Ellis. *Liturgy as a Way of Life: Embodying the Arts in Christian Worship.* Edited by James K. A. Smith. Grand Rapids: Baker Academic, 2013.

Cherry, Constance M. *The Worship Architect: A Blueprint for Designing Culturally Relevant and Biblically Faithful Services.* Grand Rapids: Baker Academic, 2010.

Drury, Keith. *The Wonder of Worship: Why We Worship the Way We Do.* Marion, IN: Wesleyan, 2002.

Maynard-Reid, Pedrito U. *Diverse Worship: African American, Caribbean & Hispanic Perspectives.* Downers Grove: InterVarsity, 2000.

Towns, Elmer L., and Vernon M. Whaley. *Worship through the Ages: How the Great Awakenings Shape Evangelical Worship.* Nashville: Broadman & Holman, 2012.

The Contextualization of Christianity

Rolando Wilfredo Cuellar, PhD[1]

> To the Jews I became as a Jew, in order to win the Jews. To those
> under the law I became as one under the law (though I myself
> am not under the law), so that I might win those under the law.
> To those outside of the law I became as one outside the law
> (though I am not free from God's law but am under Christ's law)
> so that I might win those outside the law. To the weak I became
> weak, so that I might win the weak. I have become all things to
> all people, that I might by all means save some.
>
> —1 COR 9:20–22[2]

THE UNITED STATES IS experiencing one of the greatest population booms
in its history. Through immigration and urbanization, God has brought
people from all over the world to our doorstep in North America. In response to this challenge, as Christians, we must seek understanding, not
only of the gospel message, but also of how to live out God's mission in this

---

1. Rolando Cuellar received his PhD in Intercultural Studies from Trinity Evangelical
Divinity School of Deerfield, Illinois. His professional memberships include the American Society of Missiology, Evangelical Missiological Society, Latin American Theological
Fellowship, Christian Community Development Association and the *Asociacion para la
Educacion Teologica Hispana* (AETH). He is currently an Associate Professor of Intercultural Studies at Lee University. His areas of research include the theology of immigration
and refugee, racial reconciliation, and the church as agent of individual and community
transformation. He and his wife Ruth live in Cleveland, Tennessee.

2. All Scripture quotations are from the New Revised Standard Version (NRSV) unless otherwise noted.

new context. The central thesis of this chapter is that the gospel message has been revealed to humankind in our particular cultural settings and human languages so that we can understand what God is communicating to us. The gospel has found its home in every human culture and language, but at the same time does not belong to any culture. It is in this tension between the universality and particularity of the gospel that the church must learn to interact with the themes of biblical faithfulness and cultural sensitivity. The hope is that readers will recognize the need to engage culture as part of Christian mission and theology. As disciples of Jesus Christ, we must engage in serious study of God's word, but at the same time, like the sons of Issachar, we must seek to interpret the times (1 Chron 12:32) and the cultures in which we live, so that we can know how to communicate the whole gospel, which includes salvation from sin and transformation of cultures.

What is Culture?

Nothing should be easier to define than the concept of culture for the simple reason that we all are so involved in our own cultures every day. The irony is that we often find culture very difficult to understand and define. It is like asking a fish to describe water. Unlike the fish, however, humans have created the diversity of cultures in the world. Miriam Adeney argues that God gave human beings the creativity to "develop the cultures of the world."[3] This explains the incredible diversity of cultures that exists in our communities and around the globe. The apostle Paul states boldly in his sermon to the Greek philosophers at Mars Hill, "From one ancestor he made all nations to inhabit the whole earth, and he allotted the times of their existence and the boundaries of the places where they would live" (Acts 17:26).

Before we attempt to define culture, Charles Kraft warns us about the importance to seek a better understanding of culture in three essential areas: (1) how culture has influenced us and shaped our everyday life and how we, in turn, shape culture; (2) how the culture in which the people, who we are planning to reach, live, has influenced them; and (3) how God interacts with people in the particular cultures in which they live.[4] Let us add two more areas: (4) how our understanding of the gospel message has

3. Adeney, "Is God Colorblind?", 91.
4. Kraft, *Christianity in Culture*, 46.

been shaped by the culture in which we live; and (5) how we are to communicate the gospel message within the listener's culture.

Culture is seen by Stephen Grunlan and Marvin Mayers as "learned and shared attitudes, values, and ways of behaving . . . created by the members of a cultural group."[5] Kraft defines culture as "a kind of road map . . . designed to get people where they need to go"[6] and as "a society's complex, integrated coping mechanism, consisting of learned, patterned concepts and behavior, plus the underlying perspectives (worldview) and resulting artifacts (material culture)."[7] Paul Hiebert defines culture "as the more or less integrated systems of ideas, feelings, and values and their associated patterns of behavior and products shared by a group of people who organize and regulate what they think, feel and do."[8] These integrated systems of beliefs, values, and behaviors are maps that orient us in the world and make sense to the people who live within a particular culture. This explains why, when we move from our culture to live and serve in a culture different than our own we experience cultural shock—because our cultural map does not work in other cultures. Culture plays a very influential role in our lives and, in many instances, as Christians, we are unaware of how our beliefs and ways we view the world have been shaped more by our culture than the gospel of Jesus Christ.[9]

Dimensions of Culture

To have a better understanding of culture, we need to grasp not only what culture is, but what culture does. As to what it is, culture is the system that gives direction in how people must function in a particular context. But culture as practice is expressed, experienced, and explored in what Hiebert calls the three dimensions of culture: "ideas, feelings, and values."[10]

Cognitive (Think): This dimension of culture includes knowledge that is expressed through ideas, beliefs, experiences, and language. Members of a particular culture are constantly communicating messages in several ways. Communication with one another will be impossible without knowledge.

5. Grunlan and Mayers, *Cultural Anthropology*, 39

6. Kraft, *Christianity in Culture*, 113

7. Kraft, *Anthropology for Christian Witness*, 38.

8. Hiebert, *Anthropological Insights*, 30.

9. Hiebert, *Gospel in Human Contexts*, 18.

10. Hiebert, *Anthropological Insights*, 30.

Affective (Feel): While culture has a cognitive dimension, people have affections. This dimension of culture influences our likes and dislikes and the way we express our feelings of joy and sorrow. It is also reflected in the way people dress, the food they eat, the music they listen to, and the kind of literature they read or, as in some cultures, the oral tradition.

Evaluative (Values): This dimension of culture influences our sense of right and wrong as well as what is moral or immoral. In some countries, people prefer to bend the truth somewhat, rather than hurt the feelings of those around them. In others, people tend to speak straightforwardly, regardless of whether they will offend their hearers.

According to Hiebert, "these three dimensions—ideas, feelings, and values—are important in understanding the nature of human cultures."[11] Many of us have been raised in a particular tradition, where one dimension of our culture has been emphasized more than the others, but all three dimensions of culture must be affected by the gospel for a person or community to experience genuine conversion. Let us now turn our attention to the gospel of Jesus Christ because culture must always be tested and judged by God's revelation.

What Is the Gospel?

The use of the word "gospel" in this chapter includes not only the New Testament, but also the whole Bible. I believe that God's word is inspired by the Holy Spirit, and is revealed to us for the salvation of humanity through Jesus Christ. While the gospel is eternal and universal, culture is temporal and human-made; nonetheless, God took seriously not only culture in general, but also each particular culture, because the gospel message was given to human beings living within very different cultural settings and operating on different languages. God's word originally was given to us through three different cultures and languages: Hebrew, Aramaic, and Greek, with the purpose of reconciling people to God through Jesus Christ (2 Cor 5:18). The writer of Hebrews describes the process of God's communication with us: God spoke through the prophets, but in the last days, God has spoken through his Son Jesus Christ (Heb 1:1–2). God has revealed himself to us through two important ways: his inspired word and the incarnation. While affirming these two vital doctrines, it is important to keep in mind that the gospel of Jesus was given in a particular cultural setting and linguistic

---

11. Hiebert, *Anthropological Insights*, 34.

context, and our task is to engage in the process of transporting the gospel message from its original context into a particular twenty-first-century context using familiar forms, symbols, thought patterns, syntaxes, and vocabularies to make the message understandable to local people.

The Relationship of Gospel and Culture

The relationship of gospel and culture is central to the Christian faith. This is seen in the incarnation, in which the transcendent God found it necessary to take the form of a particular human in a particular culture and time in Jesus Christ, to communicate the gospel for the purpose of the redemption of humanity (John 1:14; Phil 2:1–11). This encounter has brought tensions, and still does, as people from various cultural backgrounds respond to the gospel within their own particular historical and cultural contexts. The tension between gospel and culture is not a new problem; the early church had to face cultural issues from the very beginning of her existence. The apostles were not prepared to accept people from other cultures and ethnic backgrounds (Acts 10–11). The Council of Jerusalem is a clear example of how to solve interracial conflicts and tensions as a result of the intersection between the gospel and culture (Acts 15:1–35). When Jewish Christians threatened to impose their culture upon the gentiles who accepted Christ, the disciples offered a solution which reflected faithfulness to God's word and respect toward the culture of gentiles.

As the church grew, the early church became more open to gentiles from other parts of the Mediterranean world. The church of Antioch of Syria became the first multicultural church, by having people from different cultural settings. From this church, Paul and Barnabas were called by the Holy Spirit to take the gospel to Asia and Europe (Acts 13:1–3). Paul went and preached in Cilicia, South Galatia, Ephesus, Troas, Macedonia, Philippi, Thessalonica, Berea, Athens, and Corinth.

Like Jesus, Paul's ministry in the synagogues demonstrated his concern for the Jewish people as he tried to reach them in their own context. It was not until the rejection of the gospel by the Jewish people that Paul decided to turn his attention to the gentiles (Acts 13:46–48). Paul was sensitive in sharing Christ within the context of non-Christian cultures. The term most commonly used to describe this effort is contextualization.[12]

12. True contextualization is the expression of the gospel in local cultural contexts and familiar ways without the loss of its truth and transforming power.

This approach made Paul's message relevant and produced a profound effect on his audience; his strategy allowed him to reach different people in those cities without compromising the validity of the gospel. From Paul's missionary work, it is clear that any cross-cultural ministry goes hand and hand with immersion in local cultures.[13]

One Gospel in Diverse Cultures

Discerning the differences between the gospel and culture was and continues to be a daunting task, but it is essential for the communication of the gospel to people within their particular contexts. Too often, missionaries in the past equated the gospel with their culture. This was true, especially among Western missionaries who did not develop the need to understand the culture of the people they planned to serve. This tendency allowed them, in most cases, to see their culture as superior to the culture of others. Despite that some local customs did not have any conflict with the gospel, they were rejected and replaced by Western Christian practices. As a result, mission churches were often carbon copies of their Western missionaries' home churches, and the gospel was considered foreign. Missionaries imported their way of worship and their hymnbooks, and they even instructed local people to wear European black woolen or alpaca coats and trousers, black shoes, white shirts, black ties, and black hats.[14]

James and Lillian Breckenridge share the story of Michael Ntow, from Ghana, who recalls the time when the gospel was well-received by his people.[15] They were excited to worship this new God in ways familiar to their culture, but the missionaries brought a pipe organ. They still followed Christ, but had to accept a foreign instrument as part of their worship service. In many cases, local people rejected the gospel, not because it was not powerful enough to transform their lives, but because they considered the gospel message foreign to their local needs and culture. Using the potted plant analogy, D. T. Niles, missionary theologian from Sri Lanka, said, "Do not bring the gospel to us as potted plant, but bring it to us as seed that they germinate and grow in our soil."[16] These insights give us the opportunity to constructively consider the role of culture when presenting the gospel of Jesus Christ.

13. Luzbetak, *Church and Cultures*, 3.
14. Pobee, as cited in Hiebert, "Gospel and Culture," 202.
15. Breckenridge, *What Color is Your God?*, 42.
16. Niles, as cited in Hiebert, "Gospel and Culture," 203.

The apostle Paul assured the church of Galatia that "there is no longer Jew or Greek, there is no longer slave or free, there is no longer male and female; for all of you are one in Christ Jesus" (Gal 3:28). In doing so, Paul was focusing on both the universality and the particularity of the gospel. Paul recognized that in Christ, all walls of separation have been broken; people from every culture have become members of the body of Christ. Nevertheless, Paul was not ignoring the particular cultures and contexts in which people live. Despite the many differences between Jew and Greek, slave and free, male and female, Paul argued that we have one Lord, one faith, and one baptism (Eph 4:5).

It is essential to our mission task to present the whole gospel in familiar ways to people within their particular cultures. We must begin with the affirmation that the Bible is the inspired word of God and final authority for our beliefs and practical life. Our understanding of local cultures is important, but it should not be equated to the Bible. Even so, our mission task is to present the gospel message in truthful and relevant ways to contemporary cultures and contexts. The church in Latin America faces issues of poverty and oppression; the church in Asia deals with issues of religious pluralism, the caste system, and ancestor veneration; the church in Africa faces issues of spirits, witchcraft, magic, polygamy, and traditional religions. The church in North America deals with issues of secularization, individualism, materialism, entertainment, and violence. The presentation of the gospel cannot be divorced of culture and context. Peoples' cultures shape both their understanding of the gospel in their own cultural settings and their responses to Christ, resulting in very diverse Christian communities.

The Gospel Transforms and Redeems Culture

Jesus became incarnate in his Jewish culture, but he was also critical of his cultural, religious, and social structures of his time. Jesus declared that "his kingdom was not from this world" (John 18:36) and that his disciples were to be in this world, but not of it (John 17:14). When Jesus faced the temptations by Satan, he rejected the human desires for pleasure, materialism, and popularity which were as much part of his culture as they are of ours. In his challenge to the exclusive Jewish community, Jesus went to the synagogue of Nazareth and preached his first sermon, in which he unfolded his missionary agenda. Jesus proclaimed the inclusivity of God's kingdom when he mentioned that Elijah was sent to minister to the widow of Zarephath of

Sidon, and that Elisha healed Naaman the Syrian of leprosy (Luke 4:25–30). At the end of his sermon, "all in the synagogue were filled with rage" (Luke 4:28). The inclusion of gentiles into God's kingdom made his Jewish listeners very upset.

Jesus also summarized the entire law and the prophets in two commandments: "He said to him, 'You shall love the Lord your God with all your heart, and with all your soul, and with all your mind.' This is the greatest and first commandment. And a second is like it: 'You shall love your neighbor as yourself'" (Matt 22:37–39). An expert of the Jewish law knew very well these commands but, trying to justify himself, asked Jesus, "And who is my neighbor?" In other words, who is one of us? Jesus did not provide a definition of who is a neighbor; instead, Jesus told a story about a man who, while traveling from Jerusalem to Jericho, was beaten by thieves who left him almost dead. Both a Jewish priest and a Levite walked by showing no compassion toward this man. In contrast, a Samaritan demonstrated his concern for this man (Luke 10:25–37). Jesus presented the Samaritan as the hero of this story to challenge the ethnocentrism of his Jewish audience. For Jesus, our neighbor is anyone who is in need. This means that our love must not be limited to people who are like us, but we are called to love people regardless of their ethnic background. Our call to bear witness to the values of God's kingdom does not come without risk. Jesus himself took the risk of being accused of eating with sinners, publicans, and prostitutes (Matt 9:11) to bring them into the kingdom of God (Matt 21:31).

A significant analysis of how Christians respond to the Christ and culture dilemma was offered by H. Richard Niebuhr,[17] who suggested that there are five major paradigms: Christ against culture; Christ above culture; Christ of culture; Christ and culture in tension; and Christ the transformer of culture. One of Niebuhr's most important contributions about this dilemma is that there is no single answer to relate to a given culture. Each approach has something to contribute in regard to how a Christian must relate to culture. There are several ways of accepting, replacing, or transforming various aspects of a given culture from within. Dietrich Bonhoeffer described churches as being "in the midst of the world," as opposed to those who are "taken out of the world."[18]

For the last ten years, I have had the opportunity to travel around the world to conduct onsite visits to my Intercultural Studies students from

17. Niebuhr, *Christ and Culture*, xliii–lv.
18. Bonhoeffer, *Cost of Discipleship*, 311.

Lee University who were engaged in ten-week internships. In each of those contexts, the goodness and beauty of the image of God in men, women, and children had been made known. But I have also noticed the evidence of evil in each culture that reflects our fallen humanity. In response to this challenge, we must bear witness to the whole gospel that transforms and redeems those evil aspects of each culture that continue unchecked in much of the world, in a manner that it is consistent with the values of God's kingdom of righteousness, peace, justice, and joy in the Holy Spirit. This is an ongoing process, but we must exercise patience and love toward those who we are planning to reach. We must also do it with the conviction that God has already been at work in those cultures, establishing his kingdom where Christ is at the center.

Conclusion

The twenty-first century challenges us to develop cross-cultural ministry skills to reach out to people who come from all over the world to live in our backyards. Our God is a missionary God who has allowed the mission field to come to us. Darrell Whiteman challenges us to re-examine our Christian mission to our very diverse world when he says, "The church must take seriously differences in culture, ethnicity, gender roles, and social location if it is going to be an authentic representative of the kingdom of God on Earth. This represents a huge challenge for many Christians who strive to be culturally relevant while remaining biblically faithful."[19]

Let us look toward the future with hope and great expectation for when the relationship between the whole gospel and the diversity of cultures in our communities flourish and the church becomes very influential.

19. Whiteman, "Anthropological Reflections," 52.

Questions for Reflection

1. In your own words, how do you define contextualization?

2. What is the role of contextualization as we attempt to reach out to people outside of our culture and religion? What are the strengths of contextualization? What are the risks?

3. What are the tensions between the gospel and culture?

4. What are the lessons Jesus taught us to follow as we relate to our contemporary culture?

5. How must the church relate to the surrounding culture?

6. How do you respond to those who argue against contextualization? Please argue from a biblical/theological perspective.

For Further Reading

Adeney, Miriam. *Kingdom Without Borders: The Untold Story of Global Christianity.* Downers Grove: InterVarsity, 2009.

Gordon, Wayne. *Who is My Neighbor? Lessons Learned from a Man Left for Dead.* Ventura, CA: Gospel Light, 2010.

Lingenfelter, Sherwood, and Marvin K. Mayers. *Ministering Cross-Culturally: An Incarnational Model for Personal Relationships.* Grand Rapids: Baker, 2003.

Richards, Randolph E., and Brandon J. O'Brien. *Misreading Scripture with Western Eyes: Removing Cultural Blinders to Better Understand the Bible.* Downers Grove: InterVarsity, 2012.

The Mandate of Justice

R. Jerome Boone, DMin[1]

He has told you, O man, what is good;
And what does the Lord require of you
But to do justice, to love kindness,
And to walk humbly with your God?

—Mic 6:8[2]

The Spirit of the Lord is upon me,
Because He anointed me to preach the gospel to the poor.
He has sent me to proclaim release to the captives,
And recovery of sight to the blind,
To set free those who are oppressed,
To proclaim the favorable year of the Lord.

—Luke 4:18–19

1. Jerome Boone serves in the Department of Christian Ministries at Lee University. He is Professor of Old Testament and Christian Formation, and teaches in both disciplines. In Biblical Studies, he enjoys the rich diversity of the Old Testament as well as New Testament studies. In Christian Formation, he explores issues related to how people come to faith and how people mature in the faith. Boone teaches at both the graduate and undergraduate levels. His current research focuses on the themes of worship, justice, and creation care. He presents regularly at the annual conferences of the Society for Pentecostal Studies and has published in several journals. Boone and his wife Sandra have written discipleship curriculum on the Thanksgiving Psalms. They have two married children and four grandchildren.

2. All Scripture quotations are from the New American Standard Bible (NASB) unless otherwise noted.

THE UNEQUIVOCAL TESTIMONY OF Scripture is that God is a God of justice. The theme is so pervasive in the Bible that it is difficult to discuss it adequately in the limited space of this chapter. W. R. Brookman gives an extensive list of biblical texts related to the theme of justice,[3] demonstrating just how common it is in Scripture.

The Bible always relates justice to its contrast of injustice. The very first injustice (sin) in Scripture receives God's rebuke and judgment (Gen 3). The final injustices in human history—those described in the book of Revelation—will be punished appropriately. All the narratives in between these two events tell again and again of God's demand for justice. What is the Bible's understanding of the concept of "justice"? How is justice related to God's goal for creation? What role does humankind play in maintaining justice in the world? These are important questions for understanding a biblical perspective on justice.

This chapter will present an overview of the topic of justice from a biblical perspective. It will organize the presentation into the following subtopics: (1) justice in the Torah; (2) justice in the books of the prophets; (3) justice in the New Testament; (4) justice and benevolence; and (5) justice and the mission of the church. The discussion will be brief, but broad enough to accurately reflect the testimony of Scripture.

Justice in the Torah

The earliest stories in the Bible tell of God's justice as it is carried out in the lives of people. Cain was justly punished for his unjust murder of his brother, Abel (Gen 4). The wicked generation in Noah's day was destroyed by flood because of their sinful behavior (Gen 6:1–7). The wicked generation in Lot's time was destroyed for its unjust lifestyle and culture (Gen 19). Perhaps the greatest story of God's action against injustice is embedded in the Exodus narrative (Exod 1–15). Israel, the people of God, was unjustly oppressed in Egypt, and they cried out to God. God answered their lament with judgment on Egypt (the plagues described in Exodus 7–11). It was this significant event in the life of Israel as a nation that communicated two important truths for Israel's relationship with God: (1) God is a God of justice, and (2) God is a God of deliverance from injustice. The experience revealed an important truth about God's world: justice is God's vision for

---

3. Brookman, *Grinding the Face of the Poor*, 1–103.

the world, a world in which every creature, in community with every other creature, is seeking the well-being of others.[4]

The Exodus is the single most important historical event in the Old Testament. The revelation of God contained in the Exodus is fundamental for the rest of the Bible.[5] Justice is like a two-edged sword; it has the ability to do its work in two directions. It delivers the unjustly oppressed and it punishes the unjust oppressors. Israel was delivered from unjust oppression at the Exodus; Egypt was punished for its unjust oppression. The revelation of God was clear to both Israel and Egypt. The revelation became even more emphatic to Israel as the nation entered into covenant relationship with God at Mount Sinai (Exod 19–40).

The Pentateuch or Torah, is full of laws about justice. Many of the laws are expressed in the negative; they tell what must not be done to others. The foundational laws are the Ten Commandments. Israel is given divine commands not to murder, commit adultery, steal, tell lies, or covet (Exod 20:13–17). All of these commandments can be summarized in a single command: "you shall love your neighbor as yourself" (Lev 19:18). Beyond these fundamental laws, there are more than six hundred specific laws that instruct the people of Israel about the parameters of justice.[6] A cursory reading of Exodus 21–23 and Leviticus 17–27 will reveal examples of the hundreds of "case laws" that make up the Torah. The "case laws" deal with very specific situations and give guidance for justice. The details of all these laws make it crystal clear that the people of a just God must be just in their lifestyle as well.

Justice in the Prophets

The prophets of the eighth to fifth centuries BCE give abundant evidence that Israel did not always live according to God's covenant commandments. Amos was the earliest of the classical prophets (ca. 760–730 BCE). He condemned Israel for many injustices. Walter J. Houston[7] identifies five key passages in the prophecies of Amos that contain "a denunciation of crimes leading to an announcement of judgment" (2:6–16; 3:9–15; 4:1–3; 5:10–12, and 8:4–7). The victims of the injustices were the poor and powerless. The

---

4. Brueggemann, *Peace*, 13.

5. Martens, *God's Design*, 3–17.

6. Drazi, *Maimonides and the Biblical Prophets*, 209.

7. Houston, *Contending for Justice*, 61.

oppressors were the rich and powerful. All of these crimes were infractions of "justice [and] righteousness."[8] The issue is social justice. From an ethical point of view, oppression is an abuse of power. It is immoral even if it is legal. The motivation is often financial greed (2:6 and 5:12).[9]

Micah is another prophet who condemned the injustices of Israel. He was ministering in the southern kingdom, while Amos was active in the northern kingdom. The witness of these two prophets indicates how widespread the oppression was in ancient Israel.

Micah indicted the leaders of Israel for their failure to ensure justice. Justice is a prime responsibility of government and its leaders. It is for this reason that the apostle Paul counsels Christians to obey "governing authorities" (Rom 13:1–3). Micah said that Israel's leaders "abhor justice and twist everything that is straight" (3:9). The leaders included kings, elders, priests, and false prophets (3:9–12). Again, as in Amos, financial greed seems to be the primary motivation. The injustices of Israel would pay a price; injustice would bring about the destruction of the nation. There would be divine judgment on injustice.

Micah also took issue with injustice at the personal level. He indicted those who abused their neighbor. According to Micah, these unrighteous persons "scheme iniquity" (2:1). They covet fields and seize them, perhaps through foreclosure or illegal bribes to judges (2:2). They rob their neighbors, strip them of their clothes, and evict them from rented properties (2:2, 9). The injustices will be avenged (2:3–5). God is a God of justice.[10] God is hardwired to do justice. Any injustice draws God into the fray of human oppression as the defender of the oppressed. Therefore, Micah can remind Israel of a basic revelation from God: "He has told you, O man, what is good; and what does the Lord require of you but to do justice, to love kindness and to walk humbly with your God?" (Micah 6:8).

The other writing prophets take up the issue of social justice as well. Isaiah, Jeremiah, and Ezekiel have major discourses about it. Space limitations will not permit all these texts to be explored in detail. Amos and Micah are excellent illustrations of their fellow prophets, and must suffice for this discussion.

What we see in God's concern for justice is related to God's design for creation. The creation was designed to experience "well-being," or "shalom,"

8. Houston, *Contending for Justice*, 60–61.

9. Houston, *Contending for Justice*, 67.

10. Limburg, *Hosea—Micah*, 192.

as the Old Testament names it.[11] Unfortunately, humankind disrupted the plan. The sin of Adam and Eve—and all humankind since—resulted in consequences that mitigated against "shalom." The results of sin are such things as sickness, disease, natural disasters, and even death. The effects of sin in the world are further intensified by evil deeds of men and women. God's response to humankind's disruption is what is commonly called "redemptive work." God's redemptive work in the world is the corrective action to the consequences of sin and evil. It is God's way of moving the creation toward its original purpose.

God has a partner in the redemptive work of justice; it is humankind. Even before sin and its consequences entered the world (Gen 3), God had created humankind in God's own image to be a partner who would manage the creation (Gen 1:26–28).[12] Sin disrupted the relationship between God and the partners; but God took the initiative to resolve the problem, ultimately through Jesus Christ. In the meantime, God reconciled with those who chose to be reconciled in order to counter the effects of sin and evil.

The most significant partners of God in the Old Testament are Abraham and his descendants, a group of people known as Israel. God entered into a special relationship with Israel, called a covenant. All the laws about justice in the Pentateuch/Torah were given to Israel as guidance for doing God's will and as redemptive work in an imperfect world. The prophets were raised up by God to call Israel to do the redemptive work of God as a "light to the nations" (Isa 42:6; 49:6). Regretfully, Israel did not fulfill its destiny because of the self-centered and sinful ways of many of the people. What God had hoped for Israel is that the nations of the world would join the redemptive work of God as partners by learning about God's will and work from Israel (Isa 2:1–4). Instead, Israel was unfaithful to God's call and rebelled against God. The sad story is described in chapter one of Isaiah.

Justice in the New Testament

The failure of Israel prompted a fresh revelation of God in Jesus of Nazareth. Jesus is the clearest revelation of God ever given to the world (Heb 1:1–3). He declared what his ministry would be (Luke 4:18–19): a Spirit-anointed ministry of preaching good news, deliverance of those in bondage, help for the poor, healing for the sick and blind. The purpose

11. Brueggemann, *Peace*, 13–15.

12. Brueggemann, *Genesis*, 32–33.

was to restore well-being (shalom) to God's creation. One way to describe Jesus' ministry is to portray it as a hugely enhanced redemptive work of God; a greater work than had ever been experienced by humankind.[13] In fact, it was the beginning of the kingdom of God on Earth. The work of the kingdom would assault the works of sin and evil, overcoming them (Matt 16:18). The kingdom of God is real, but not physically identifiable. It has no geographical borders on planet Earth. In a sense, it is a realm of reality where God's will is done on earth as it is heaven.[14] It is a place where the reign of God rules supreme. The entire New Testament is given to the story about the arrival of God's kingdom in Jesus of Nazareth and its expansion to the people groups of the world.

In essence, the people who come to faith in Jesus Christ become the new, spiritual Israel.[15] They have the same mission as that which God gave to Israel. This is most obvious in the similarity of the wording of God's declaration about Israel in Exodus 19:5–6, and of the church in 1 Peter 2:9–10.

> But you are a chosen race, a royal priesthood, a holy nation, a people for God's own possession, so that you may proclaim the excellencies of Him who has called you out of darkness into His marvelous light; for you once were not a people, but now you are the people of God; you had not received mercy, but now you have received mercy.

Just as God expected Israel to be a light to the nations (Isa 42:6), the church is expected to illuminate God's character and will in its life and witness. Therefore, the matter of justice is an important issue in the redemptive work of God in which the church participates. The New Testament is filled with stories and exhortations about justice. The fresh revelation of God in Jesus of Nazareth reaffirms God's interest in justice. When Jesus was asked to identify the "greatest" commandment of God, he immediately reiterated the earlier revelation in Deuteronomy 6:5: "You shall love the Lord your God with all your heart and with all your soul and with all your might" (Matt 22:37). But Jesus did not stop there. He quickly repeated another earlier revelation to ancient Israel found in Leviticus 19:18: "you shall love your neighbor as yourself" (Matt 22:39). The word "love" in this statement is a verb; it requires action more than emotion. The commandment is expressed in a different form in Matthew 7:12: "In everything, therefore, treat

13. Dempsey, *Justice: A Biblical Perspective*, 104–5.

14. Wright, *Simply Christian*, 91–103.

15. Powell, *Introducing the New Testament*, 473–74.

people the same way you want them to treat you, for this is the Law and the Prophets." It is more commonly known as the "golden rule" in this passage. The main point is this: Jesus identified the "greatest commandment" from God as one that includes being "just" (loving) towards others.

When the church continued the redemptive work of God after Jesus was resurrected and ascended back to heaven, it sought to practice justice (or, love) toward others. This is evident in the narrative of the book of Acts. The early church included many widows who needed assistance with adequate food supply (Acts 6:1–6). The good news is that the church provided for the widows. The bad news is that there was an unjust distribution of the food. The narrative indicates that the Jewish widows were given more food than the Hellenist widows. The Hellenist widows complained about the injustice. The church corrected the situation quickly because the apostles knew God's will about injustice.

Carol Dempsey says that "one of the greatest works of justice for the sake of peace was Jesus' message to and work among Gentiles."[16] The narrative of the book of Acts describes how the early church extended the gospel of Jesus to gentiles throughout the Roman Empire. The Apostle Paul was the primary evangelist of the good news to gentiles.[17]

James, in his epistle to the church, addressed another form of injustice (2:1–9). The injustice focused on extending privilege or special consideration to those who are wealthy.[18] Honoring the wealthy over the poor is unfair; it is unjust. It would not be difficult or inappropriate to apply this principle to any situation where one group is given privilege over another group based on social or economic differences. James' corrective to this injustice was to remind the Church of God's commandment: "If, however, you are fulfilling the royal law according to the Scripture, 'You shall love your neighbor as yourself,' you are doing well" (2:8).

Justice and Benevolence

Justice alone cannot offset the impact of sin in the world. There are many people who are suffering from the consequences of impersonal forces such as drought and famine, or storms and destruction. Life circumstances like disease and accidents can create much suffering. The redemptive work

16. Dempsey, *Justice: A Biblical Perspective*, 106.

17. Dempsey, *Justice: A Biblical Perspective*, 106–7.

18. Powell, *Introducing the New Testament*, 457–59.

of God must include benevolence as a complement to justice. Benevolence is the work that seeks well-being (shalom) for all people, regardless of the source of the problem. Benevolence is not unconcerned with the source of the problem; it simply addresses needs without concern for the root cause. For this reason, Micah can describe what God expects of humankind as doing justice and loving mercy (benevolence) (6:8). Carol Dempsey characterizes this aspect of justice as "compassion."[19] She addresses it as the necessary complement of justice.

The story of Ruth (chapters 1–4) is an excellent illustration of the relationship between justice and benevolence. Ruth and her mother-in-law, Naomi, were both widows. After their husbands died, they moved to the town of Bethlehem. Ruth voluntarily took on the responsibility to care for Naomi. She lived in a farming community, so she decided to provide food by "gleaning" (Ruth 2). Gleaning was allowed by Israel's law in order to allow poor people access to food supply (Lev 19:9–10; Deut 24:19–22). According to the law, poor people could come onto the property of any farm and harvest the produce that was left after the owner's workers had completed their harvest. Ruth worked on a farm owned by Boaz. Boaz was a righteous man and allowed Ruth to glean on his property just as the law required. Moreover, he warned his male workers not to molest Ruth who was very vulnerable as she worked in the fields. In addition to being just toward Ruth, Boaz instructed his workers to leave extra grain for her when she was gleaning near them (Ruth 2:14–16). This was an act of benevolence. Boaz allowed grain that was "lawfully" his to be given to Ruth. Boaz knew of Ruth's good works toward Naomi, and he wanted to help Ruth.

The just and benevolent character of Boaz became even more evident when he decided to correct an injustice being done to Ruth.[20] According to Israelite law (Deut 25:5–10), any widow who was childless should be given in marriage to the nearest male relative of her deceased husband. The law relates to what is called "levirate marriage." It was a legal procedure designed to care for younger widows who would otherwise be prone to poverty. Ruth was poor and gleaning for food because her deceased husband's relative had not committed to marry her and care for her. Boaz took action to correct this injustice. He went to the town elders (where legal matters were adjudicated) and insisted that Ruth be given justice. The man who had responsibility to care for Ruth was identified and confronted. The man re-

---

19. Dempsey, *Justice: A Biblical Perspective*, 87–99.
20. Hubbard, *Book of Ruth*, 231–62.

fused to marry Ruth. In an act of justice and benevolence, Boaz volunteered to marry Ruth. He also agreed to care for Naomi. The book of Ruth ends on this resolution. In the context of the "days of Judges," a spiritually dark time in Israel's history, the virtue of Ruth and the just and benevolent character of Boaz stand out like diamonds on a black velvet cloth.

Justice and the Mission of the Church

The overview of a biblical perspective on justice and benevolence given above raises important questions for people of faith. What does God expect from us when it comes to justice and benevolence within our own world? Does God's goal for all creation, including humankind, continue to be "well-being" (shalom)? Are we God's partners in the quest for the world's well-being? Is this responsibility personal, or is it a job for the church? The answers to these questions are critical for discipleship. They will shape how today's disciples of Jesus will live their lives.

The answers to all these questions are related to God's mission in the world today, the *missio Dei* as it is commonly called. God is at work in the world today in redemptive ways, continuing to move the world towards the consummation of the kingdom of God on Earth. The redemptive work of God is the focus of the mission of the church. Consequently, the redemptive work of God is both the corporate mission of the church and the individual mission of disciples of Jesus. The answer to Micah's question ("What does the Lord require of you?") is just as important for the church and contemporary disciples as it was for Israel: "do justice, love mercy [benevolence] and walk humbly with your God" (6:8). The prophet Zechariah reminded Israel of just how important justice and benevolence are to God (7:8–14). While justice and benevolence are not the totality of what God is doing in the world today, it is a major component of the *missio Dei*.

Ronald Sider contends that, when asked about what the gospel means, most western-society Christians answer "forgiveness of sins."[21] He agrees that the gospel includes the forgiveness of sins, but emphasizes that the gospel message of Jesus is about so much more. Jesus' ministry focused on teaching, preaching and healing. He sought justice and well-being for the poor and oppressed. He fed the hungry and welcomed the socially ostracized. He lived what he taught as a visible demonstration of the reality of the kingdom he inaugurated. Sider strives to encourage Christians to move

21. Sider, "What if We Defined?", 25.

to a more holistic mission that reflects Jesus' own message of the kingdom of God.[22] Reconciliation must transform social and economic relationships within the community of faith. Ministry must address the social and physical needs of people, not just their spiritual needs.

God's concern for the well-being of humanity is most often described in the Bible as concern for the poor, widows, orphans, and strangers. It is a concern for those who do not have the necessary resources for good health and safety. It is estimated that two-thirds of the world's population fit into this category. The challenge of seeking well-being for so much of the world's population can be overwhelming. The solution rests in God alone; a God for whom nothing is impossible. But God has chosen not to act without God's people. It is the people of God who must participate in God's mission. God's people, made in the image of God, are partners in the creation. The statement echoes the purpose of God expressed in the creation narrative (Gen 1:26–28).

Some people have argued for the redemptive consequences of certain political or economic systems as a solution to the world's needs. They contend that God is at work providentially in democracy, monarchy, capitalism, or socialism to resolve the world's problems. As Daniela Augustine has convincingly pointed out: "The Eastern European experience has proven that neither socialism nor capitalism holds the answer to solving issues of economic justice and sustainability in the world."[23] The answer is not found in human institutions or social systems because all such systems presuppose certain values or priorities. No human system is value-neutral.[24] All such political and social systems privilege certain classes of people and specific values. Even the best of human social systems is vulnerable to the influence of greed.

The goal of God for all humanity is human flourishing. Miroslav Volf emphasizes the importance of understanding a biblical view of what it means to flourish.[25] He contends that contemporary Western culture has redefined flourishing as limited to mere satisfaction. Historically, human flourishing was centered on God and the attributes of God's people. The shift to experiential satisfaction of the self can never give an adequate sense of meaning to life. Human beings need to know, on an intellectual level, the reason for being in order to enjoy life. Without that sense of purpose, life

---

22. Sider, "What if We Defined?", 28–30.

23. Augustine, "Holiness and Economics," 176.

24. Augustine, "Holiness and Economics," 171–73.

25. Volf, "Human Flourishing," 14–17.

loses all sense of meaning.[26] Volf addresses the question of how can human flourishing be united with the biblical revelation of God? He believes that God's people need to make plausible the claim that love for God and love for neighbor will result in human flourishing.[27] This proposition must be a fundamental belief of the community of faith if it is to be a reality.

The only sustainable solution is the transformative power of God that changes the default human choice rooted in self-centeredness to one that loves the other as much as the self. The goal of this transformation is evident in the so-called land laws of the Torah and their concern for the poor and marginalized. The concrete testimony of the reality of this transforming power is preserved in the early chapters of the book of Acts. The coming of the Holy Spirit on the day of Pentecost (Acts 2) radically altered the community of faith. Spirit-filled disciples of Jesus were transformed. The outcome was a community that shared resources and made sure that everyone had their needs met (Acts 2:42–47; 4:32–37).

Conclusion

Douglas Meeks[28] was my first significant encounter for understanding the economics of God's creation. His insightful book initiated a journey that has shaped my perspective of the Christian faith over many years. Justice is an important theme everywhere in the Bible in both Testaments. In the beginning, all creation was just. The fall of humankind dramatically changed the world. Now, the people of God must participate in the redemptive work of God to renew the world according to the will of God. We must begin with the prayer that Jesus taught his disciples to pray: "Your kingdom come, your will be done, on earth as it is in heaven," (Matt 6:10). Then, we must allow the Spirit to illuminate our comprehension of the injustices and human needs around us. The Spirit knows God's will for human flourishing in each person's life. As Van Gelder says, we must be governed by the word of God as we are led and taught by the Spirit of God.[29] As we submit to the power of the Spirit at work within us, we will be the transformed partners of God doing the *missio Dei*. We will fulfill our vocation as the called and sent people of God.

26. Volf, "Human Flourishing," 19–25.
27. Volf, "Human Flourishing," 30.
28. Meeks, *God the Economist*.
29. Van Gelder, *Essence of the Church*, 142–46.

Questions for Reflection

1. How does the Pentateuch/Torah emphasize that God is a "God of justice"?

2. What is the role of humankind in God's redemptive work of justice among the peoples of the Earth?

3. Where is Jesus' concern about justice evident in his ministry?

4. Why was the early church concerned about justice? How is this concern evident in the New Testament?

5. How is justice complemented by benevolence?

6. What is the relationship of justice to the mission of the church?

For Further Reading

Brookman, W. R., ed. *Grinding the Face of the Poor: A Reader in Biblical Justice.* Minneapolis: North Central University Press, 2006.

Donahue, John R. *Seek Justice That You May Live: Reflections and Resources on the Bible and Social Justice.* Edited by David Hollenbach. Mahwah, NJ: Paulist, 2014.

Lints, Richard. *Renewing the Evangelical Mission.* Grand Rapids: Erdmans, 2013.

Lowe, Ben. *Doing Good Without Giving Up: Sustaining Social Action in a World that's Hard to Change.* Downers Grove: InterVarsity, 2014.

Meeks, M. Douglas. *God the Economist: The Doctrine of God and Political Economy* Minneapolis: Fortress, 1989.

Woolnough, Brian, and Wonsuk Ma. *Holistic Mission: God's Plan for God's People.* Eugene, OR: Wipf & Stock, 2010.

The Process of Inculturation

Edley J. Moodley, PhD[1]

The Word became flesh
and made his home among us.
We have seen his glory,
glory like that of a father's only son,
full of grace and truth.

—John 1:14[2]

ACCORDING TO THE LATEST statistics on the status of world Christianity produced by the Center for the Study of Global Christianity, 2.48 billion of the world's 7.52 billion people today embrace Christianity in its varied forms as their religious faith.[3] Its linguistic accessibility, ethnic diversity, and universal appeal make Christianity the largest cultural movement in the

---

1. Dr. Moodley serves as Director of the Intercultural Studies Program and Professor of Intercultural Studies at Lee University. He is a graduate of the E. Stanley Jones School of World Mission and Evangelism, Asbury Theological Seminary, Wilmore Kentucky, with a PhD in Intercultural Studies. Dr. Moodley, prior to emigrating to the United States in 1994, served the church in South Africa in various administrative roles and pastorates for more than twenty years. In the area of Christian education, he taught at Bethesda Bible College and founded a Bible training institute, Aletheia Bible College, for lay people in Durban, South Africa, in 1989. He joined the faculty at Lee in 1999. Dr. Moodley has traveled to more than eighty countries of the world on six continents as conference speaker, missions educator, and preacher. His monograph *Shembe Ancestors and Christ: A Christological Inquiry with Missiological Implications* was published in 2008.

2. All Scripture quotations are from the New Revised Standard Version (NRSV) unless otherwise noted.

3. Johnson, "Christianity 2017," 41.

world. Today, more people, more languages, and more diversity in liturgical styles and worship patterns than the world has ever known characterize the Christian church. These factors that demonstrate not only the reason for the exponential growth of the church, but also the ensuing impact of Christianity across the globe, are attributed to the process of inculturation, the birthmark of the church since its inception.

Christianity, though cradled in Jewish culture early in its history, became a pluralist dispensation, admitting to its ranks all who vowed allegiance to the person of Jesus Christ—confessing Christ was the only litmus test, not dependent on cultural affinity (Gal 3:28). Thus, the universality or catholicity of the gospel is contingent upon the process we call inculturation. This essay will first examine the church as God's inculturating agency to the world; second, a brief discussion of the term inculturation will follow; third, we will explore the theological motif of the incarnation as a model for inculturation; fourth, we will look at inculturation through the lens of the New Testament; fifth, we will make a case for Christianity as a vernacular translating movement; and sixth, we will draw a contrast between Christianity and Islam where any translation of the Qur'an is denied divine sanction by its adherents.

The Character of the Church

When we understand the church's role in the world from the perspective of theology, ecclesiology, and missiology, we have to say that the church is God's mission to the world.[4] In the aftermath of the death of Jesus and his subsequent resurrection, Jesus said to his disciples, "As the Father has sent me, so I send you . . . receive the Holy Spirit" (John 20:21–22). Commenting on the words of Jesus, Karl Barth—the Swiss Protestant theologian (1886–1968)—in his paper presented at the Brandenburg Missionary Conference (1932) argued that the Latin term *missio* (send/sending) was understood as an expression of the doctrine of the Trinity in the early church. He went on to explain that mission is the divine sending of self, the Son, and the Holy Spirit to the world.[5]

However, it would only be at the 1952 Willengen Conference of the International Missionary Conference (IMC) that the idea of the *missio*

4. Moltmann, *Church in the Power of the Spirit*, especially the section "Participation of the Church," 64–65.

5. Thomas, *Classic Texts in Mission & World Christianity*, 105–6.

Dei (Mission of God) received a more distinct articulation: "The classic doctrine of the *missio Dei* as God the Father sending the Son, and God the Father and the Son sending the Holy Spirit was expanded to include yet another 'movement': Father, Son, and Holy Spirit sending the church into the world."[6] David J. Bosch, in his magnum opus, would further argue that "there is church because there is mission, not vice versa."[7] In a similar vein, Emil Bruner stated, "The church exists by mission, just as fire exists by burning. Where there is no mission there is no church."[8] Thus, to my mind, when we speak of the mission of the church, we recognize first and foremost that God is the initiator and sustainer of his mission (*missio Dei*), and that he invites us to participate as his instruments when he sends us— his church—into the world. Second, the practical outworking of the above is that the church's mandate is to function in this world as witness to God's sovereign reign of love, salvation, justice, and *shalom*, thus fulfilling the Triune God's agenda for the whole cosmos.

Even a casual reading of the New Testament will reveal the multiplicity of symbols and images employed to describe and define the church. These symbols and images include the body of Christ, the people of God, the church of God, "vine" or "vineyard," the bride of Christ, the elect, the new creation, members of the household of God, "priesthood," "servant," and "herald," among many others. In his classic study *Models of the Church*, Catholic theologian Avery Dulles describes various ways of envisioning the church. Couching the New Testament symbols for "church" in six models (institution, community, sacrament, herald, servant, and school of discipleship), Dulles defines the fundamental functions of the church, characterizes its mission in the world, and explores the church's multiple roles in the lives of believers—a useful study indeed.[9] The varicolored tapestry of images, metaphors, and models provide a truly kaleidoscopic view of the richness of the church. Thus, no one image is superior to the other.

However, without detracting from the significance and usefulness of these images—given that they are not mutually exclusive, but dependent on each other and intimately related—the most lucid for our missiological,

---

6. Bosch, *Transforming Mission*, 390. Bosch was the missionary theologian of the twentieth century whose enduring work in *Transforming Mission: Paradigm Shifts in Theology of Missions* is still the definitive text in mission theology to this day.

7. Bosch, *Transforming Mission*, 390.

8. Bruner, *Word and the World*, 108.

9. Dulles, *Models of the Church*. Also see Snyder, *Liberating the Church*, especially his chapter "Liberating Models of the Church," 96–146.

theological, and ecclesial understanding in this study is the description of the church as the body of Christ (Rom 12:4–5; 1 Cor 12:13; Eph 1:23; 4:4, 12; Col 1:18–24). Barth uses the "body of Christ" symbol in communitarian language when he says, with reference to Jesus, "As His earthly-historical form of existence, the community is His body, His body is the community."[10] In his communion model, Dulles also depicts the church as the "body of Christ," one that grows "into the final perfection of the Kingdom."[11] While on Earth, the church is never complete, but always exists in a state of becoming. As Christ's body, the church is sent into the world, propelled and motivated by the Holy Spirit for its mission, and its sole mission according to Snyder is "to be the First fruits of the Kingdom, present now, as Jesus was, in humility and service."[12] The key to the church's relevance today is precisely when it lives for its non-members; or in the words of Bonhoeffer, "The Church is the Church only when it exists for others."[13] In the final analysis, mission "is the good news of God's love, incarnated in the witness of a community [church], for the sake of the world."[14] The process of inculturation has been made possible in the proliferation of the "good news" to humankind and continues unabated even today by the community we call the church.

Defining the Term "Inculturation"

Although this term has gained universal reception and is widely used by missionary theologians today, it nonetheless is of more recent vintage. Gregorian University professor J. Masson, SJ was the first to use the term in a theological sense in 1962.[15] Fr. Pedro Arrupe, SJ (the twenty-eighth superior general of the Society of Jesus—an organization known for its rigorous scholarship and apostolic zeal) defines inculturation as "The incarnation of Christian life and of the Christian message in a particular cultural context, in such a way that this experience not only finds expression through elements proper to the culture in question . . . but becomes a principle that animates, directs and unifies the culture, transforming it and remaking it so

---

10. Barth, *Church Dogmatics*, 666.

11. Dulles, *Models of the Church*, 89.

12. Snyder, *Liberating the Church*, 109.

13. Bonhoeffer, *Letters and Papers*, 203–4.

14. Bosch, *Transforming Mission*, 519.

15. Bosch, *Transforming Mission*, 447.

as to bring about a new creation."[16] Using the qualitative method of research among members of an African church, African theologian Laurenti Magesa found that respondents repeatedly defined inculturation as "a process by which the word enters the people's lives so that they practice it in their everyday life."[17] From these definitions, we gather that inculturation may be deemed to be a continuing conversation between faith and culture(s). Such a dialogue is never static, but always dynamic, changing as new elements are introduced into the conversation.

The Christian faith has the potential to take on the character of the context in which it manifests itself without diminishing the essence of the gospel message or the cultural norms of a people. Thus, any attempt at inculturation must of necessity begin with the translation of the gospel into the local idioms and forms. The question of translation of the Scriptures, discussed later in this essay, will reveal the legitimacy and value of the African church's commitment to the process of inculturating the gospel.

The Incarnation as Model for Inculturation

From the perspective of missiological anthropology, the terms inculturation and incarnation are sometimes used synonymously referring to the "process by which a local church integrates the gospel message (the 'text') with its local culture (the 'context')."[18] The fusing of the text and context results in what Luzbetak calls "Christian living."[19] While there is much to say about incarnation as a theological interpretation of missionary reflection and practice, I want to draw attention to the historical incarnation event as a model for inculturation.[20]

In his Gospel, the apostle John tells us that God, who is Spirit (4:24), is the same God who "became a human being and lived among us" (1:14, Phillips)—a missional motif "of God moving into the flesh, *in carnus*."[21]

---

16. Shorter, *Toward a Theology of Inculturation*, 11.

17. Magesa, *Anatomy of Inculturation*, 38. The Qualitative Method of Research uses participant observation, in-depth interviews, and focus groups for obtaining a specific type of data.

18. Luzbetak, *Church and Cultures*, 69.

19. Luzbetak, *Church and Cultures*, 69.

20. See for example, Guder, The Incarnation and the Church's Witness (Pennsylvania: Trinity Press, 1999).

21. Luzbetak, *Church and Cultures*, 2.

God taking on human flesh, blood and bone, crossing the time and space barrier, and coming to live among a fallen, fallible people in the person of Jesus Christ is an apt paradigm for inculturating the gospel.

The context of our Lord's entry into this world is graphically illustrated in Luke's Gospel (2:1–20). Jesus came as a helpless child born in a manger. He did not come as a fully developed adult, nor did he come with any kind of authority or superior pedigree. In fact, he came as an infant in a lesser known culture and a subjugated land. We know also that he came as learner, in that, as an ordinary child, he had to learn the Hebrew and local languages and culture. He lived under the authority of his artisan parents (2:51) and learned the trade of a carpenter from Joseph. He studied the Scriptures with the rabbis of his day (2:46) and perhaps had some kind of a rite of passage akin to the *bar mitzvah* at the age of 13. He attended all the religious ceremonies mandated for Jews, including temple and synagogue services (4:16). He was subject to the law like any other Jew (Gal 4:4). In fact, Jesus studied the culture and the Hebrew Scriptures for thirty years before he began his public ministry. While inculturation as a model for disseminating the "good news" has its genesis and its legitimacy in the mystery of the incarnation, there is also the indispensable dimension of humility and selfless dedication that the Christian advocate needs to demonstrate in the work of ministry.

Paul's Christological Hymn, sometimes referred to as the "Kenotic Theory of the Incarnation" (Phil 2:5–11), provides a worthy paradigm for humble obedience and service: "though he was in the form of God, He did not regard equality with God as something to be exploited. . . . [He] emptied himself, taking the form of a slave, being born in human likeness. And being found in human form, he humbled himself and became obedient to the point of death—even death on a cross" (2:6–8). In this passage, Paul declares that Christ in his incarnation emptied (*kenosis*) himself of his glory in order to identify completely with humanity. In so doing, he established a model for mission that displays a "bold humility" rather than a belligerent triumphalism.[22] The incarnation of Jesus (as model) and the kenotic mystery of Christ (as historical example) thus become exemplary for the praxis of inculturating mission and ministry.[23]

22. Hall, *Thinking the Faith*, 22–33.

23. Baillie, *God Was In*, 94–98. Notwithstanding the critique of the "kenotic theory" from Baillie, the theory suggests that the divine Logos, or second person of the Trinity, laid aside his divine prerogatives and attributes (omniscience, omnipotence, and omnipresence) and was subject to human limitations like all human beings.

Inculturation in the New Testament

Inculturation as a model differs from its predecessors (i.e. adaptation, accommodation, and contextualization models), in that the principal participants responsible for incarnating the gospel are members of the indigenous local community and the Holy Spirit. However, this model does not preclude or mitigate the role of the sending church or, for that matter, the universal church ("outsiders"). Regarding the latter, Schreiter rhetorically asks, "Is a local church willing to stand under the judgment of other churches in the matter of its Christian performance or does it close itself off, assured of its own truth?"[24]

The history of the church is the strongest argument for inculturation. If one of the key agents in the inculturation process is the Holy Spirit, the New Testament offers the historical precedent in the book of Acts, one that sets the stage for the universalizing of the Christian faith. Luke sets this inaugural event in the context of the conversion of the Roman army officer, Cornelius (Acts 10:1—11:18). Cornelius was a "God-fearer" who, having resisted all formal allegiances to Roman and Greek gods and goddesses, embraced Second Temple Judaism and its austere monotheistic faith. However, Cornelius had accepted the Jewish faith only up to a point, thus avoiding many cultural distinctives which, while sacred to the Jew, were abhorrent to the Roman in the first century. Some of the imperatives included restrictions to certain foods and their preparations, keeping the Sabbath, and participation in the various festivals. However, the most significant ritual observance was circumcision—the defining cultural issue that separated gentiles from Jews, including the fledgling Jewish Christ followers.[25]

In response to the question regarding circumcision as the litmus test for salvation, by divine intervention Cornelius is encouraged to extend an invitation to Peter, who would testify that the only way to salvation is through Jesus Christ—"he will give you a message by which you and your entire household will be saved" (Acts 11:13–14). Simultaneous with Cornelius's epiphany, Peter is visited by the Holy Spirit, and in a vision he is asked to eat four-footed animals and birds and pay Cornelius a visit in his home in Caesarea (11:9–23). Peter's initially bold remonstrations finally turn to humble obedience when the Holy Spirit gently nudges him with a

---

24. Schreiter, *Constructing Local Theologies*, 119–20. See also Moodley, *Shembe Ancestors and Christ*, 204.

25. McKnight, *Light Among the Gentiles*, 45–48, 78–82.

revolutionary announcement: "What God has made clean, you must not call profane." Peter's response is, "I truly understand that God shows no partiality" (10:15, 34). This paradigm shift in Peter's understanding resulted in what missiologists refer to as Peter's second conversion—a cultural conversion. Luke is careful to record the role of Holy Spirit in both the experience of Cornelius and Peter, who needed conversion so that the mission of God would be advanced both locally and globally.

If the universal mission of God's salvation announced by Simeon (Luke 2:32) was to become fully realized, the cultural supremacy exerted by the early Jewish Christians had to be annulled.[26] The forum for this momentous decision was the Jerusalem Council, where Peter convincingly recounts the visions both he and Cornelius experienced (Acts 15:7–12), and Peter recalls, for their benefit, how God had reoriented his religiocultural thinking and beliefs. However, it is the apostle James who makes the final argument in support of the gentile mission—a mission without any precondition or captivity to cultural supremacy. He astutely cites the Scriptures (Amos 9:11–12) as prophetic fulfillment of the time when "all other peoples may seek the Lord—even all the Gentiles over whom my name has been called" (Acts 15:16–17) and enter the kingdom without the yolk of Jewish cultural bondage placed upon them.

The case for inculturation is clearly evident in this case study (Acts 15). If authentic inculturation is to take place in a given context, both "receiver" and "sender" have to concede certain aspects of their cultures that they deem expendable. In this Jewish/gentile case study, note that Christian Jews had to concede that cultural and sociological criteria, as mandated in the Mosaic law, should not be required for gentile converts, because "Luke's Jesus has separated salvation from Torah, or at least has found a way to include gentiles without first making them Jews."[27] On the other hand, gentile Christians (the receiving culture) had to concede some cultural traits so as not to offend Jewish sensibilities. Gentile Christians had to refrain from sacrificing to pagan gods, incestuous marriages, eating meat from strangled animals, and ingesting blood.[28] Thus the process of inculturation, one that is authentic and true to the gospel, will include as its principal participants the host or receiving culture (insiders), the sending culture (outsiders), and the Holy Spirit, as is evident in this Jewish/gentile case study.

---

26. Senior and Stuhlmueller, *Biblical Foundations for Mission*, 273.

27. Willimon, *Acts*, 130.

28. Willimon, *Acts*, 130.

Christianity: A Missional Movement

Lamin Sanneh, professor of Missions at Yale Divinity School, who has ably documented the path Christianity took to adopt translatability from the very early stages of its history, suggests that culture is "the natural extension" of the fledgling religion—a religion which was cradled in Judaism—so much so that "cultural failure [was deemed to be] entirely incompatible with Christian success."[29] It naturally followed that the fledgling Christian faith was able to forge "a critical interface with the cultural materials it encountered."[30] We know from history that the early church had to compete with superior world cultures for its survival to become a world religion—not least among them was the dominant culture of Imperial Rome.[31] The safeguard against idolatry to any one culture is evidenced in the plurality of the Christian faith stemming from the ease of translatability it enjoyed even in the face of Judaization, Hellenization, and Westernization.

Koine Greek became the medium of literary and scholarly writing in the latter part of fourth-century BCE following the conquests of Alexander the Great, and it became the *lingua franca* of the Byzantine Empire. *Koine* became the language of the Septuagint—the third-century BCE translation of the Hebrew Bible—and, very early in Christianity's sojourn to becoming a world religion, writers of the New Testament used the Greek language effectively to communicate the Christian gospel.

John, the Gospel writer, in the prologue (John 1:1–18) for example, employed the *logos* concept from Greek literature and philosophy, investing it with Christian meaning. The term had several shades of meaning in Greek literature and philosophy, and primary among them, the *logos* concept referred to "the divine reason, the controlling principle of the universe."[32] The fourth gospel is one example of the process of inculturation advancing the cause of the faith with the infusion of local indigenous concepts. Christianity, a faith cradled in Judaism, could claim universality on the basis of the ease of translatability, both linguistically and culturally, as evidenced in the history of the church and its sacred text, the Bible.

29. Willimon, *Acts*, 130.

30. Sanneh, *Discipling the Nations*, 29.

31. See Niebuhr, *Christ and Culture*. The author developed a five-part theoretical framework for analyzing the relationship between church and culture.

32. Sanneh, *Discipling the Nations*, 61.

Islam: A Contrasting Movement

Muslims believe that the Qur'an is a mediated message from God via the Angel Gabriel to Muhammad; the first message Muhammad receives is recorded in chapter (sura) 96. It begins with the word "Recite!" (*iqra* in Arabic), which is the same Arabic root as *qur'an*. Thus, the Qur'an is a book of "recitations," containing the very thoughts of Allah, and the medium of communication was the Arabic language. For Muslims, the language of the Qur'an is unlike any of the languages of the world, claiming the capacity to resist difference and historical precedent, because only such a language is worthy of the God who spoke it. That Muslims ascribe to Arabic the status of a "revealed" language is borne out by several Qur'anic verses (10:38–39; 11:1–2; and 16:104–5, among others). The internal logic is that the author of the Qur'an is God, and that God reveals himself to humankind through the book—the Qur'an.

The implications of a non-translatable Qur'an for its adherents, especially non-Arabic speaking Muslims is enormous. It is mandatory for Muslims, including non-Arabic Muslim converts, that when ritual acts of worship (*salat*), fasting (*sawm*), and the pilgrimage to Mecca (*hajj*) are performed, the liturgical utterances emanating from the lips of Muslims when enacting these rituals, are always in Arabic. Thus, mother-tongue speakers find themselves in an unenviable position, where the revered status of Arabic disenfranchises the vernacular. Native speakers thus implicitly concede that their own languages are relegated to irrelevancy.

If, as it has been argued, that the early church, "in straddling the Jewish-Gentile worlds was born in a cross-cultural milieu, with translation as its birthmark," the stark contrast is seen in Islam, in that its birthmark lies in its Arabic linguistic hegemony, as evidenced in the non-translatability of the Qur'an.[33] Consequently, the Islamic claim that the Qur'an is God's final revelation to humankind, superseding the Bible, denies its very *raison d'etre*—the very reason for its existence—given the fact that Arabic is spoken by a minority in the world today.

It is inconceivable that a faith destined for the world and the vehicle for God's final revelation to humankind would be confined to one minority language in the world. A cultural and linguistic oddity indeed! The contrast between Christianity and Islam cannot be more clearly defined, in that the early church adopted the principle of inculturation through cultural and

33. Bosch, *Transforming Mission*, 458.

linguistic phenomena at its disposal; not least among them was the fact that Christianity—although cradled in Judaism—elevated no one culture or language above others. This is evident in the Pentecost event, when women and men assembled in Jerusalem testified of God in their vernacular tongues (Acts 2). The mission of the church is and always will have as its ultimate goal the inculturation of the gospel, if it is to be true to its Lord and his command (Matt 28:18–20).

Conclusion

At the very outset, we said that inculturation is defined as dialogue between the gospel message and a new culture. Yet, we also come to understand that inculturation is more than just that—it is the gospel incarnating or bringing to birth a new cultural creation. When Jesus is fully realized in a local culture, new and creative ways of living and expression of faith in Christ become evident. We have learned that Christianity, as contrasted with Islam, became a translating movement: first, translation of the Scriptures to meet the need of local speakers, as contrasted with Islam, where the Arabic language is considered the revealed language and, therefore, untranslatable; second, very early in its formation, the church relinquished Jerusalem as its religious center, whereas Islam has consecrated Mecca as its sacred space with its yearly pilgrimage; and third, the church was able to assimilate into the Greek and Hellenistic cultural milieu and adopt Greek philosophical categories, thus making the gospel message relevant in that culture. As we have seen, Islam, for its part, requires Arabic as it was first revealed, to be the language for worship and devotion. The relevancy of the Christian faith today lies in its unique ability to be an inculturating activity in the world, given that culture is dynamic and always changing. While Christianity transcends culture, the Christ of Christianity has the ability to incarnate in any given culture.

Questions for Reflection

1. Discuss your understanding of the term "inculturation," and suggest its relationship to the theological term "incarnation." Use biblical texts to support your thinking on this subject.

2. Construct a narrative in which you demonstrate your understanding that the Hebrew Scriptures and Jewish culture in which Christianity was born were merely "surrogate," not the message itself. Use biblical evidence to present your argument.

3. The primary goal of the gospel-culture encounter is to assist people in coming ever closer to God. Suggest ways this chapter has helped you come to that understanding.

4. From your reading of the chapter, what would you consider critical entities for the process of inculturation to take place in a given culture?

5. Contrast Islam and Christianity by suggesting ways that one is a translation movement, while the other is not.

For Further Reading

Magesa, Laurenti. *Anatomy of Inculturation: Transforming the Church in Africa*. Maryknoll: Orbis, 2004.

Mattson, Ingrid. *The Story of the Quran: Its History and Place in Muslim Life*. Malden, MA: Blackwell, 2008.

Niebuhr, Richard H. *Christ and Culture*. New York: Harper & Row, 1951.

Sanneh, Lamin. *Translating the Message: The Missionary Impact on Culture*. Maryknoll: Orbis, 1996.

Shorter, Alyward. *Toward a Theology of Inculturation: Transforming the Church in Africa*. Maryknoll: Orbis, 2004.

The Preservation of Creation

R. Jerome Boone, DMin[1]

The earth is the LORD's, and all it contains,
The world, and those who dwell in it
For He has founded it upon the seas
And established it upon the rivers.

—Ps 24:1–2[2]

HAVE YOU DISCERNED THE grand narrative of the Bible? Have you noticed the way the Bible begins and ends? The metanarrative from Genesis to Revelation is all about the creation. Genesis begins by describing the creation "in the beginning" (Gen 1–2). Revelation ends by focusing on the "new" creation coming at the end of human history (Rev 21–22). Between these two important creation stories, the fall and redemption of all creation is the primary narrative. Too often we think of the Bible as concerned only with the redemption of humankind. Not true; Paul declares

1. Jerome Boone serves in the Department of Christian Ministries at Lee University. He is Professor of Old Testament and Christian Formation, and teaches in both disciplines. In Biblical Studies, he enjoys the rich diversity of the Old Testament, as well as New Testament studies. In Christian Formation, he explores issues related to how people come to faith and how people mature in the faith. Boone teaches at both the graduate and undergraduate levels. His current research focuses on the themes of worship, justice, and creation care. He presents regularly at the annual conferences of the Society for Pentecostal Studies and has published in several journals. Boone and his wife, Sandra, have written discipleship curriculum on the Thanksgiving Psalms. They have two married children and four grandchildren.

2. All Scripture quotations are from the New American Standard Bible (NASB) unless otherwise noted.

in Colossians that "for by him [Jesus] all things were created, in heaven and on earth . . . For in him [Jesus] all the fullness of God was pleased to dwell, and through him [Jesus] to reconcile to himself all things, whether on earth or in heaven, making peace by the blood of his cross" (Col 1:15–20). To the Romans, he says, "For the creation waits with eager longing for the revealing of the sons of God. For the creation was subjected to futility, not willingly, but because of him who subjected it, in hope that the creation itself will be set free from its bondage to corruption and obtain the freedom of the glory of the children of God" (Rom 8:19–21). This deliverance will happen when Jesus returns to establish his kingdom on Earth.[3]

It is that time between the original creation and the re-creation that concerns us in this chapter. It is a time period in which humankind has a very important role to play. The well-being of all of creation depends on men and women doing what God created them to do. The responsibility given to humankind is the preservation of God's creation.

The role of humankind from the beginning has been to be God's partner, or steward, in caring for and managing the creation.[4] The narrative of the creation account makes this clear (Gen 1:26–28). When Adam and Eve were created, they were placed in the Garden of Eden to care for the garden (Gen 2:15). Even though the created world at that time was unaffected by the effects of sin, it needed to be managed and cultivated. The entry of sin into the world had a huge impact on the creation, as well as on the core being of humankind. Sin brought with it the corruption of the world in which people live, and of the very nature of humankind.

The time period between the entry of sin and its effects on the world, and the radical restoration of all things at the Second Coming of Jesus, is the focus of God's redemptive work. The phrase "God's redemptive work" is commonly used to describe God's activity aimed toward countering the consequences and effects of sin and evil.[5] God's activity is sometimes by direct intervention into human history (e.g., the Genesis flood, Israel's Exodus from Egypt, Jesus of Nazareth, etc.). However, most often God's activity is "providential," working through nature and human agency. It is the providential work of God that utilizes people in every generation to assault the forces and consequences of sin and evil.

---

3. Sider, "Biblical Foundations," 46.

4. Weaver, "Co-Redeemers," 199.

5. Van Gelder, *Essence of the Church*, 30–31, 88–90.

The providential work of God in the world is not limited to God's people. It can work through any person because God is sovereign over all people. The goal of God's redemptive work is always the well-being (frequently referred to as *shalom*) of all creation. The Psalms and wisdom literature of the Hebrew Bible illuminate this particular work of God. Psalm 148 calls upon every aspect of the creation—heavens, angels, sun, moon, stars, storms, snow, clouds, mountains, rivers, animals, fish, birds, all people, and specifically Israel—to give praise to God for his creation and preservation of the world. God, in his response to Job, surveys the daily workings of the world. God's discourse emphasizes the stability of the world in his providential care for the creation (Job 38—41). Job is humbled by the overwhelming evidence of God's work in the world, and can only declare that he has spoken to God without understanding (Job 42:1–3).

Jesus often used illustrations of God's providential care for the creation in his teachings (e.g., Matt 6:25–34). There seemed to be no dispute, even from his enemies over this fact. The apostle Paul expressed his full faith in the providential work of God in his sermon at Athens (Acts 17:24–28). He summed up the discourse by declaring that, in God, "we live and move and have our being." The Bible is filled with references to God's faithful, ongoing work of sustaining the creation.

God's providential preservation of creation is often accomplished through God's partners—humankind. The covenant people of God play a special role in this work. *Shalom*, or well-being, can only exist when God's will is being done. Once this is understood, the importance of care for creation takes on significance. How can people and all the rest of creation experience well-being if the creation is polluted with toxins? Or, how can all people and the rest of creation have well-being if some aspect of the population is destroying the Earth's resources (e.g., food supply). The whole issue of creation care takes on a broader perspective when justice issues are considered. Calvin DeWitt contends that "human beings have become the predominant destructive force on earth."[6] He argues that human destruction of the Earth is greater than the damage caused by floods, earthquakes, and hurricanes. Even some Christians participate in the destruction of the creation as a result of focusing only on Christ the Redeemer at the expense of God the Creator.[7] To be sure, care for creation is directly related to justice and benevolence from a biblical perspective. Consequently, creation care

6. DeWitt, "Creation's Environmental Challenge," 61.

7. DeWitt, "Creation's Environmental Challenge," 63–64.

has a direct relationship to one of the two greatest commandments: "love your neighbor as yourself" (Mark 12:31). Care for creation is an activity in which we demonstrate a concern for the interest of others (Phil 2:4), as well as an expression of worship for the Creator (Ps 8).

Creation Care and God's Covenant People

Israel is the "covenant people" of God in the Old Testament. Abraham was the first recipient of a covenant that provided special access to God for him and his descendants. The focus of the Old Testament (Hebrew Bible) is on this people group. Israel's unique relationship with God gives us insights about the responsibility of God's people for the preservation of creation. The nation of Israel received its foundational revelation from God after the Exodus from Egypt. The essence of that revelation has been canonized in the Torah (the Pentateuch). Within this revelation, there are many stipulations about how to care for the creation (i.e., land, animals, other persons, etc.).

The land laws, in the Torah of the Hebrew Bible, are stipulations about how ancient Israel was to use the land given to them by God. The land of Canaan was promised to Abraham and his descendants as part of their covenant with God (Gen 13). Even though land was God's gift to Israel, God remained the sovereign owner of it.[8] Continued possession of the land of Canaan was predicated on obedience to the will of God. Covenant obedience required that the land be used as God stipulated. One of the important regulations about land was the requirement to let the land rest every seven years (Sabbath years, Lev 25) as well as every fiftieth year (Jubilee years, Lev 25). This rest affected both the land and the people. It was intended to be a time of restoration and renewal. Sandra Richter[9] has written an excellent article which provides details of land renewal.

God's continuing ownership is also evident in the laws about tithing (Num 18). The tithe, a tenth portion, was the rightful property of God. It was the payment due to the ultimate land owner.[10] The tithe was God's legitimate portion, and anyone who refused to give it was considered a thief (Mal 3). What exactly did God do with God's tithe? God used the tithe to

8. Martens, *God's Design*, 120–24.

9. Richter, "Environmental Law," 363–65.

10. Richter, "Environmental Law," 358–61. Sandra Richter gives a strong historical and cultural defense for this understanding of Canaan as God's land.

support and provide for God's ministers, the priests and Levites (Num 18). It was also used every third year to help provide for the poor (Deut 14).

The land laws reveal the goal of creation care to be well-being for all of God's creation. The Sabbath and Jubilee years were not merely rest for land, animals, and people; they were to be times of human flourishing. Those in bondage were to be set free. Slaves were to be released and debts were to be annulled (Deut 15). It was a "fresh start" for those in poverty. The Jubilee year had a special provision for the restoration/redistribution of land back to the original tribes that were given the land of Canaan. In Israel's agrarian economy, land was the primary source of wealth creation. Well-being was closely related to owning land. God was concerned that land not become the sole possession of a limited group of people. Land was a blessing. It could be bought and farmed for profit. It could generate wealth for its owners. But it could not be kept in perpetuity by enterprising landowners. The Jubilee year required a reallocation of land to emerging generations every fifty years.

One of the most important land laws relates to "gleaning" (Lev 19, 23, Deut 24 and Ruth 1–4). The law for gleaning required every landowner to share the produce of the land with the poor.[11] The book of Ruth is based on a story in which "gleaning" is well illustrated. Ruth and her mother-in-law were both widows. As such, they were struggling to survive. In order to have an ample food supply, Ruth would go to the fields of Boaz and glean the grain. According to the land laws, the landowner could not harvest a field, vineyard or orchard more than one time. So farmers always waited until their harvest was at its peak before they sent their workers to harvest. During the harvest, grain that was too ripe or not ripe enough was left in the field. People who needed food (e.g., widows, orphans and immigrants) could come to any field that a farmer had harvested and gather what was left. No special permission was needed from the landowner. A principle is very evident in the provision for gleaning: what the land produces must be shared with those in need.

There are other seemingly odd laws in the Torah that relate to creation care.[12] Israel is instructed not to cut down fruit trees during warfare as a material for siegeworks (Deut 20:19–20). Non-fruit bearing trees may be used for military purposes but not fruit trees. Fruit trees often take many years to replace, because some do not bear fruit for ten to twenty years after the tree is planted. Another odd law concerns killing a mother bird and

11. Merrill, *Deuteronomy*, 324.
12. Fretheim, *God and World*, 138–39.

taking its eggs (Deut 22:6–7). The eggs may be taken if the mother bird is spared. As different as this law is from the law against destroying fruit trees, there is a common denominator: the means of life and food production must be preserved. Boundaries must be set to prevent the exploitation of creation.[13] The implications for creation care are obvious.

The New Testament does not take up the issue of creation care in the same manner as the Old Testament. Some of the reasons for this is that the historical-cultural context of the New Testament is very different than that of ancient Israel. Yet the New Testament advocates for creation care as a means of honoring the Creator. There is no doubt that abusing and polluting the environment dishonors the Creator. Moreover, it is an injustice against humanity.

Creation Care and the Glory of God

Creation care is more than a compassionate response to those who live in poverty, or at the margins of society; it is a response to who God is. God is the Creator.[14] God created the heavens and the earth and all they contain. The psalmists of ancient Israel often reflected on this truth. God as Creator is the focus of Psalms 8, 19, 24, 95, 104 and 148. The psalmists simply expand on the story of creation in Genesis 1–2. The wisdom literature finds confidence in the stability of life evident in the creation. God not only created the heavens and the earth, he sustains the creation through his providential care (Job 38—41; Prov 8; Eccl 3). The prophet Isaiah uses creation theology to encourage the Israelites living in the Babylonian exile to hope in the power of their God to restore them (40–55). Creation theology is a major theme throughout the Bible. It is a motive for worship of the Creator God.

The New Testament focuses on Jesus as the God-man and participant in creation. The Gospel of John declares that Jesus, the Word of God, was there in the beginning. All things were created through him (John 1:1–5). Paul says that, since the creation of the world, God has been evident to all humankind through God's eternal power and divine nature (Rom 1:30). Paul advances this thought in the letter to the Colossians; he proclaims that Jesus is the One through whom all things were created. All power and authority over the creation has been delegated to Jesus (Col 1:15–20). The writer to the Hebrews concurs (Heb 1:1–2). Jesus, as a member of the triune

13. Fretheim, *God and World*, 139.

14. Moltmann, *God in Creation*, 77–103.

God, created and sustains all of creation. Moreover, God is reconciling all creation through Jesus Christ (Col 1:20).

The role of Jesus as "reconciler" of all creation defines the redemptive work of God in an important way for Christians. As people made in the *Imago Dei* ("image of God"), Christians already have the responsibility of being God's partners in the management of creation. Now, as covenant partners with Jesus Christ, there is the added responsibility to work toward the reconciliation of all things to God. The faithful disciples of Jesus could be described as co-redeemers, as they continue the redemptive work toward the coming of the kingdom of God in its fullest manifestation. In this perspective, redemptive work is proleptic; it moves history toward God's kingdom.[15] In this work, Christians are taught to pray: "Thy kingdom come, Thy will be done, on earth as it is in heaven" (Matt 6:10).

What becomes apparent in this perspective is that the preservation of creation brings glory to God. Care for creation is a means of honoring God the Creator. Care for creation is more than an attempt to save planet Earth. It is an effort aimed at reconciling the creation to God's original purpose: a hospitable habitat for all living things. The goal is well-being, or *shalom*, for all of creation. The eschatological goal is beautifully described in Isaiah 65:17–25. God's vision for a reconciled creation is prophesied as coming to reality in Revelation 21–22. The glory of God inherent in these prophetic messages should become our motivation for caring for creation. However, truly caring about the creation will take more than momentary inspiration. As Peter Harris has noted, "This is a change or a development in the depth of our relationship with God himself."[16]

Developing a Plan to Care for Creation

Many faith traditions have not emphasized a care for creation attitude in their discipleship process. Consequently, many contemporary Christians do not embrace the preservation of creation as a vital aspect of their Christian commitment. There are a number of reasons for this oversight about creation care. First, the New Testament is focused on redemption theology much more than on creation theology. It clearly recognizes God as Creator of all things, but the emphasis is on the redemptive work of God for humankind in Jesus Christ. The emphasis is not surprising, given the significance

15. Moltmann, *God in Creation*, 4.

16. Peterson et al., "Joyful Environmentalists," 30–32.

of the work of Jesus. However, the work of God as Creator must not be separated from the role of God the Redeemer. Both characterizations of God are equally true of the Trinitarian God.

Second, the context for most North Americans is urban. The church in North America ministers to people who have little contact with nature—except perhaps during vacations. As a people group, North Americans do not spend much time thinking about the beauty and awesome character of the creation. It may be that we are too far removed from the awesomeness of the creation to be impressed. When we survey the landscape, what we see is mostly the creation of human beings: tall commercial buildings, attractive homes, automobiles, well-developed cityscapes. Even at night, the bright lights are not the moon and stars. If anything, the city lights obscure the moon and stars. In some instances, the cityscapes are drab and dirty. The dwelling places are slums. Nothing in such a neighborhood suggests the glory of God. Consequently, the church must help Christians understand the creation as much greater than their limited dwelling space.

Third, the mission of the church often gets itemized and prioritized. When this happens, spiritual aspects of God's redemptive work get emphasized at the expense of other aspects of mission—things like evangelism, feeding the hungry, worship services, etc. Whatever the reason, many Christians do not give much attention to creation care. But, this oversight can be and should be corrected.

The key issue is this: what can we do to change our perception of the Christian life, as well as our habits and our actions, to more fully care for creation? How can we live our Christian lives in ways which are more faithful to God as both Creator and Redeemer? Developing a proper attitude about caring for creation begins with worship—specifically, worship of God as Creator. The fact that God created the heavens and the earth, and all that is in them (Ps 24:1–2), means that all things belong to God. All of creation is not just created by God; it is created for God as well (Col 1:16). The creation is God's own possession and he cares for every part of it (Ps 104). The well-being of the creation is directly dependent on the benevolence of its Creator. Therefore, it is not surprising that one of the motivations for worship and praise in the Psalter is gratitude. Psalm 148 summons all of creation to give praise to its Maker and Sustainer.

The most obvious way in which the contextualization of the Psalter for creation theology is evident is the liturgical call to worship. Psalm 95 illustrates the perspective well (vv. 1–7). Creation is a motive for worship. Israel, individually and corporately, as well as many other aspects of creation, are called to worship God, the Creator and Sustainer of life (Ps 33, 148). The worship called for is what could be termed a rightful response in view of the covenant concept related to creation. The vertical relationship of creatures/creation to Creator deserves a response of gratitude and worship. Human beings are described as the crown of creation in Psalm 8; but when it comes to worship of the Creator, they stand side by side with the rest of creation.

Worship of God as Creator must be complemented by a vision of God's will for creation. Look again at the revelation about the goal of God for creation expressed in Isaiah 65:17–25 and Revelation 21–22. The prophetic revelation should be our own guiding light for doing creation care. The critical question is: What can we do, in the power of the Spirit, to move creation toward this vision? The answer begins with a biblical vision of creation; it is well-being for all creation.

The community of faith must understand the relationship between the redemptive work of God in Jesus Christ and the role of God as Creator. God created the world as a place of supportive environment for all creation—human and non-human. God created humankind to be God's partners in creation to nurture, and manage the creation in a way that will ensure well-being (*shalom*) for every aspect of the creation.

Each community of faith must seek to know the needs of the world around them in order to construct a plan for doing God's redemptive work. The redemptive work will always move the creation in the direction of its consummation at the second coming of Jesus. The following is a sample of redemptive activities that push back against the consequences of sin and evil in order to restore the creation to a supportive environment.

- Begin with your own community of faith and talk with the leaders of your church. Ask the pastor to preach specific sermons on caring for creation. Encourage the church's discipleship leader to include curriculum on caring for creation.

- Create a partnership with a local church or school to sponsor activities which will contribute to making the environment a more supportive place to live. Many communities are willing to participate in what is commonly called a three R's program (reduce the use of Earth's resources, re-use products instead of discarding them, and recycle materials to save on Earth's resources).

- Organize a clean-up project to remove litter from highways, streams, or parks in order to preserve the well-being of the environment.

The activities listed above are only a few of the things that can make a difference in our world. The list reflects those things that can be done in most communities to care for creation. Many other activities can be found with a simple internet search. The logistics of how to organize and carry out most of the activities is readily available on the internet. The important thing is to do something!

Worship and vision must be accompanied by prayer and action. God is at work in the world all around us all of the time. In prayer, we discern how God is at work so that we can get in step with it.[17] We seek the empowerment of God's Spirit to do kingdom work. As faithful disciples, we pray for God's will to be done on Earth as it is in heaven. It is in the matrix of worship, vision, prayer, and action that we experience the kind of transformation that changes the depth of our relationship with God and opens the way for genuine care of creation.

Conclusion

The preservation of creation must be an aspect of responsible Christian discipleship. Its neglect in some faith traditions is unfortunate. The twenty-first century has witnessed a major shift in attitude toward this omission. Many faith traditions that formerly ignored creation care are now giving attention to it. Leaders in the work of ministry have an opportunity to illuminate the importance of caring for God's creation. The preservation of creation relates directly to the "great commandment" (Mark 12:29–31). Love for God leads to the worship of the Creator. Gratitude for what God does in sustaining the creation is a proper motive for worship. The rightful response to God's sovereign care for all of creation is joyful worship. From this perspective, how can we not be moved to care for creation? How can we not join in God's mission to redeem the creation from the effects of sin?

The Great Commandment includes love for one's neighbor as an expression of love for God. Care for creation has a major impact on neighbors. The land laws of the Old Testament testify to the important role that the creation plays in achieving well-being for the world. Creation produces the resources that support life. These resources must be protected and managed.

17. Blackaby and King, *Experiencing God*, 52–57.

The destruction of creation's resources, through unmanaged consumption or pollution, will result in the destruction of life. God is a God of life. God's will is for all of life to experience well-being. How can we not care for creation as a means of loving our neighbors? How can we not join the efforts to preserve the resources of God's creation in order to sponsor life and well-being?

Questions for Reflection

1. How does the grand narrative of the Bible begin and end in the context of Genesis to Revelation? Relate the opening and closing themes of the Bible's grand narrative to the redemptive work of God.

2. Where is the key biblical text in Genesis that describes God's purpose for humankind in creation? Discuss the biblical role of humankind in the care of creation.

3. How do the key aspects of the land laws of the Old Testament (e.g., Sabbath years, gleaning, etc.) relate to care for creation?

4. Why does caring for creation help to fulfill the great commandments (Mark 12:29–31)?

5. What is the relationship between creation theology and redemption theology in the grand narrative (metanarrative) of the Bible?

6. Where are the needs in your local community that could be addressed by care for creation activities? Create a plan to carry out three such activities.

For Further Reading

Berry, Robert James. *The Care of Creation: Focusing Concern and Action*. Downers Grove: InterVarsity, 2000.

Bouma-Prediger, Steven. *For the Beauty of the Earth: A Christian Vision for Creation Care*. 2nd edition. Grand Rapids: Baker Academic, 2010.

LeQuire, Stan L, ed. *The Best Preaching on Earth: Sermons on Caring for Creation*. Valley Forge, PA: Judson, 1996.

Lowe, Ben. *Green Revolution: Coming Together to Care for Creation*. Downers Grove: InterVarsity, 2009.

Sleeth, J. Matthew. *The Gospel According to the Earth: Why the Good Book Is a Green Book*. New York: HarperOne, 2010.

Toly, Noah J., and Daniel I. Block, eds. *Keeping God's Earth: The Global Environment in Biblical Perspective*. Downers Grove: InterVarsity, 2010.

Commissioning

So we return to our opening question, "What is the mission of the Church?" Theologian Emil Brunner might respond to this query with his oft quoted statement, "The church exists by mission as a fire exists by burning."[1] One might ask Brunner, "How does fire combust in the first place?" Here is a possible answer. Jesus was a radical arsonist; he ignited fires everywhere and simply asked whoever might follow after him to keep his Messianic fires aflame. At some point in history, entire churches exchanged their birthright of being cultural and ecclesiological igniters of His Spirit for a calling that has sadly resulted in questionable theology, predictable programming, an institutional herd mentality, unbridled internal backbiting and cultural blindness.

My colleagues and I stand on the conviction that there will be no advance of the Kingdom of God which does not encompass first an authentic personal conversion through repentance and faith in the Lord Jesus Christ.[2] *The authentic personal conversion experience begins with church leaders.* It should be underscored that the primary quest of the Church is not to increase membership, build more impressive facilities, open another food pantry, or offer the finest worship services available to its local constituents. The first missional aspect of the church and of the life of any believer is the exaltation of Jesus Christ. Remembering Jesus' words: "When I am lifted up I will draw people unto myself."[3]

While reflecting on final thoughts for this publication I was taken back to my days as a young believer. In the words of writer Tommy Tenny, I was a *God Chaser.*[4] As a new follower of Jesus, I read 'the red' daily and looked

---

1. Emil Brunner, quoted in Steve Timmis and Tim Chester, *Gospel-centered Church* (Good Book, 2002), p. 10.

2. 2 Chronicles 7:14

3. John 12:32

4. See Tenny, Tommy, *The God Chasers*; Destiny Image publishers. 1998

for ways to serve others. While engaged in street ministry in the red light district in Hollywood, California I witnessed great pain and heard stories of people who were willingly and wildly living apart from God. As those in the United Sates dealt with their own personal heartaches, I encountered my own desolation abroad as a twenty year old missionary to South Korea. For a brief summer season, far from home for the first time, I was confronted with starvation conditions. On one occasion, I saw a young mother leaving her earthen dwelling in the early morning to bury her infant child who had died in the night. Later that same evening I read these words from scripture, "Is it nothing to you, all you who pass by? Look around and see . . ."[5] In thinking about these memories and many others, I asked myself during the final writing of this manuscript, "Do I still have the same clarity of vision and depth of passion that I had as a new believer?" I share my intimate inner questions about vision and passion because vision and passion are easily corrupted and forgotten.[6]

Jesus' mission commenced when he identified with humanity.[7] *And so it should be with the mission of the church today.* Jesus recognized temptation, hunger, thirst, love and betrayal at the deepest of extremes. These are all basic component parts of today's humanity. "In bringing many sons to glory, it was fitting that God . . . should make the author of their salvation perfect through suffering." "Because he himself suffered when he was tempted, he is able to help those who are being tempted."[8] Church advancement today occurs as the body of believers lives out the incarnation of Christ in a personal, communal and concrete way.

Jesus' identified mission was developed further as he met both the physical and spiritual longings of people. *And so it should be with the church today.* If a person was in need of grace, Jesus offered that.[9] When a desperate father came to Jesus because his son required healing, he demonstrated his healing power.[10] If people were hungry, Jesus fed them.[11] If clear teaching was needed, Jesus taught.[12] When people expressed an interest in follow-

5. Lamentations 1:12

6. See Revelation 3:4,5

7. John 1:1; Hebrews 1:2

8. Hebrews 2:10,18

9. John 4:1-30

10. Luke 9:37f.

11. Matthew 14:13-21

12. Mark 6:6

ing him, Jesus extended an invitation.[13] Any time an individual or entire church body responds to the physical, spiritual, individual, or corporate needs before them, the mission of the original first century church is reenacted and replicated.

An additional facet of Jesus' mission was his sending forth his disciples to do the very works that he was performing.[14] Jesus' followers were to be seen as extensions of himself. *And so it should be with the church today.* Jesus declared that when anyone feeds the hungry, welcomes the stranger, clothes the naked, cares for the sick and visits the prisoner, this would provide evidence of a person's true identity as a believer upon his glorious return.[15] This notion of doing the works of God was further developed by the Apostle Paul.[16] Paul taught the believers at Corinth and Ephesus that God bestows differing gifts; no one person can do everything. Just as a body has diverse elements with each serving a different function, so it is with individual lives in the church body.[17] In some way, all Christians are called to be witnesses,[18] and all are called to love their neighbors.[19] As a final reminder related to doing the works of God, Jesus prophetically declared, ". . . whoever believes in me will do the works I have been doing, and they will do even greater things than these, because I am going to the Father."[20] What an encouragement this is!

Jesus made it abundantly plain that the primary reason he wanted his followers to believe his teaching, follow his example, and do the works that he did was that "the world may believe."[21] The gospel writer John clearly embraced the importance of this notion of believing. John stated, as he concluded his gospel, that the very purpose for his writing was that " . . . you would believe that Jesus was the Messiah, the Son of God, and that by believing in him you might have life."[22] This is Jesus' ultimate goal and mission-belief in him. *And so it should be with the mission of every church.*

13. Luke 9:57f.

14. Luke 10:1f.

15. Matthew 25:31-46

16. 1 Corinthians 12; Romans 12 and Ephesians 4

17. 1 Corinthians 12:12

18. Matthew 10:32

19. Matthew 22:36; Mark 12:31

20. John 14:12

21. John 17:21

22. John 20:31

When the church is faithful to the life and teaching of Jesus,[23] preserves the unity of the believers,[24] is both deliberate and intentional about being immersed in community,[25] the church becomes the most powerful force for drawing those who have yet to hear and accept the Good News of the Gospel.

The guiding purpose of this book is to unmistakably state that the mission of the church is multi-faceted. The mission of the church is advanced when a church perceives itself as an instrument of God and thereby acts an agent of change in the culture in which it finds itself. Citing the initial image of fire referenced at the outset of this conclusion, the church is NOT set ablaze when believers gather together, but rather when God's people are dispersed throughout the world and throughout the week.

One cannot know if the early disciples ever fully understood Jesus' mission before the coming of the Holy Spirit. Peter's question to Jesus before our Lord's ascension and before Pentecost, "Lord, are you at this time going to restore the kingdom to Israel?"[26] leads us to think Peter still did not understand Jesus' wider understanding of Kingdom. Peter is still thinking, little "k". Jesus' kingdom is a Kingdom that goes beyond politics, geography, gender, ethnicity or denominational preferences. Just a short time *after* Jesus ascends into heaven the historian and gospel writer Luke records angels from heaven calling out to those gathered, "Men of Galilee, why do you stand here looking into the sky? This same Jesus, who has been taken from you into heaven, will come back in the same way you have seen him go into heaven."[27] This angelic question is in actuality a mandate, a charge, a commissioning for the forward movement of what Jesus had begun. The angels were in effect saying, "It's time to get to work." The work may be the work of anticipatory prayer, or of fellowship or of any number of needful concerns given the circumstances.

A final question may be helpful at this time. Is today's church much like the pre-Pentecost men of Galilee who were caught up in star gazing? Were these pre Pentecost leaders, like today's church, more concerned with

23. John 8:31

24. Jesus' final prayer in John 17 clearly shows his deep heart and concern for relational unity and its impact on the furtherance of the Kingdom, "May they experience perfect unity that the world would know that you sent me and that you love them as much as you love me".

25. John 17:14,15; Romans 12:1,2

26. Acts 1:6

27. Acts 1:11

filling a leadership vacancy[28] than waiting in anticipation for the promised Holy Spirit? The mission of the church today is to be looking for the bright morning star.[29] Today's church is called to live in anticipation of Jesus' second coming. Until Jesus' coming, the church is to know that She is the empowered bride of Christ, fully capable of doing the very works her resurrected lord prophesied. You might have noticed that this final writing, traditionally titled, "Conclusion" is not a conclusion. But rather, this final piece of writing is titled, "Commissioning." Yes, it is time. It is far later than anyone of us can imagine. It is time to begin, at a deeper level, the mission to which Jesus called us.

28. Acts 1:26
29. Revelation 22:16

Bibliography

Adeney, Miriam. "Is God Colorblind or Colorful? The Gospel, Globalization, and Ethnicity." In *One World or Many? The Impact of Globalization on Mission*, edited by Richard Taplady, 87–104. Pasadena: William Carey Library, 2003.

———. *Kingdom Without Borders: The Untold Story of Global Christianity*. Downers Grove: InterVarsity, 2009.

Adewuya, J. Ayodeji. *Holiness in the Letters of Paul*. Eugene, OR: Cascade, 2016.

American Heritage Dictionary. Boston: Houghton Mifflin, 1991.

Anderson, Ray S. "Christ's Ministry Through His Whole Church." In *Theological Foundations for Ministry*, edited by Ray S. Anderson, 6–22. Grand Rapids: Eerdmans, 1979.

———. *The Shape of Practical Theology: Empowering Ministry with Theological Praxis*. Downers Grove: InterVarsity, 2001.

Augustine, Daniela C. "Holiness and Economics: Towards Recovery of Eucharistic Being in a Market-Shaped World." In *A Future for Holiness*, edited by Lee Roy Martin, 171–204. Eugene, OR: Wipf & Stock, 2013.

Baillie, D. M. *God Was in Christ: An Essay on Incarnation and Atonement*. London: Faber and Faber, 1968.

Barna, George. *A Fish Out of Water: 9 Strategies Effective Leaders Use to Help You Get Back into the Flow*. Nashville: Integrity, 2002.

———. *Growing True Disciples*. Colorado Springs: Waterbrook, 2001.

———. *What Americans Believe: An Annual Survey of Values and Religious Views in the United States*. Ventura: Regal, 1991.

Barna Group. "Six Reasons Young Christians Leave Church." https://www.barna.com/research/six-reasons-young-christians-leave-church/.

———. "Three Trends on Faith, Work and Calling." https://www.barna.com/research/three-trends-on-faith-work-and-calling.

Barth, Karl. *Church Dogmatics: The Doctrine of Reconciliation*. Translated by G.W. Bromily. Edinburgh, UK: T. & T. Clark, 1958.

Baxter, Richard. *The Reformed Pastor*. Richmond: John Knox, 1956.

Bayles, Bob, and Timothy K. Beougher. "Richard Baxter: Educating Through Pastoral Discipleship," In *A Legacy of Religious Educators: Historical and Theological Introductions*. Lynchburg, VA: Liberty University, 2017.

Beach, Charles. "Is The Bible Really True?" Lecture presented at Lee College, Baytown, TX, September 10, 1996.

Benson, Bruce Ellis. *Liturgy as a Way of Life: Embodying the Arts in Christian Worship*. Edited by James K. A. Smith. Grand Rapids: Baker Academic, 2013.

Berry, Robert James. *The Care of Creation: Focusing Concern and Action*. Downers Grove: InterVarsity, 2000.

Blackaby, Henry T., and Claude V. King. *Experiencing God*. Nashville: Broadman and Holman, 1994.

Blanchard, Ken, and Phil Hodges. *Lead Like Jesus*. Nashville: W. Publishing Group, 2005.

Bolsinger, Tod E. *It Takes a Church to Raise a Christian: How the Community of God Transforms Lives*. Grand Rapids: Brazos, 2004.

Bonhoeffer, Dietrich. *The Cost of Discipleship*. New York: Simon & Schuster, 1959.

———. *Letters and Papers from Prison*, edited by Eberhard Bethgy. New York: Macmillon, 1967.

———. *Life Together*. San Francisco: HarperOne, 1978.

Boone, Jerome. "Worship and the Torah." In *Toward a Pentecostal Theology of Worship*, edited by Lee Roy Martin, 5–26. Cleveland: Centre for Pentecostal Theology, 2016.

Bosch, David. *Transforming Mission: Paradigm Shifts in Theology of Missions*. Maryknoll, NY: Orbis, 1991.

Bouma-Prediger, Steven. *For the Beauty of the Earth: A Christian Vision for Creation Care*. 2nd edition. Grand Rapids: Baker Academic, 2010.

Bradshaw, Timothy. *Praying as Believing: The Lord's Prayer and the Christian Doctrine of God*. Macon, GA: Smyth & Helwys, 1998.

Breckenridge, James, and Lillian Breckenridge. *What Color is Your God? Multicultural Education in the Church*. Grand Rapids: Baker, 2003.

Brookman, W. R., ed. *Grinding the Face of the Poor: A Reader in Biblical Justice*. Minneapolis: North Central University Press, 2006.

Brueggemann, Walter. *Genesis: Interpretation: A Bible Commentary for Teaching and Preaching*. Atlanta: John Knox, 1982.

———. *Peace*. St. Louis: Chalice, 2001.

Bruner, Emil. *The Word and the World*. London: SCM, 1931.

Carrasco, Rodolpho. "A Pound of Justice: Beyond Fighting for a Just Cause." In *An Emergent Manifesto of Hope*, edited by Doug Jones, 247–58. Grand Rapids: Baker, 2007.

Carson, D. A. "When is Spiritually Spiritual? Reflections on some Problems with Definition." *Journal of the Evangelical Theological Society* 37.3 (September 1994) 381–94.

Chand, Sam. *Bigger, Faster Leadership: Lessons from the Builders of the Panama Canal*. Nashville: Thomas Nelson, 2017.

———. *Leadership Pain: The Classroom for Growth*. Nashville: Thomas Nelson, 2015.

Cherry, Constance M. *The Worship Architect: A Blueprint for Designing Culturally Relevant and Biblically Faithful Services*. Grand Rapids: Baker Academic, 2010.

Cross, Terry. *Answering the Call in the Spirit: Pentecostal Reflections on a Theology of Vacation*. Cleveland: Lee University Press, 2002.

Culpepper, Raymond E. *The Great Commission Connection*. Cleveland: Pathway, 2011.

Daffe, Jerald. *Clothing a Naked Church*. Cleveland: Pathway, 2010.

———. "An Introduction to Worship of Bible College Ministerial Students." DMin diss., Western Conservative Baptist Seminary, 1983.

Davies, Rupert. *Westminster Dictionary of Christian Theology*. Edited by Alan Richardson and John Bowden. Philadelphia: Westminster, 1983.

Dempsey, Carol J. *Justice: A Biblical Perspective*. St. Louis: Chalice, 2008.

DeWitt, Gavin. "Creation's Environmental Challenge to Evangelical Christianity." In *The Care of Creation*, edited by R. J. Berry, 61. Downers Grove: InterVarsity, 2000.

Dickens, Charles. *A Tale of Two Cities*. London: Chapman and Hall, 1859.

Dodds, Adam. "The Mission of the Spirit and the Mission of the Church: Towards a Trinitarian Missiology." *Evangelical Review of Theology* 35.2 (2011) 209–26.

Donahue, John R. *Seek Justice That You May Live: Reflections and Resources on the Bible and Social Justice*. Edited by David Hollenbach. Mahwah, NJ: Paulist, 2014.

Downs, Tim. *Finding Common Ground: How to Communicate With Those Outside the Christian Community . . . While We Still Can*. Chicago: Moody Bible Institute Press, 1999.

Drazi, Israel. *Maimonides and the Biblical Prophets*. Jerusalem: Gefen, 2009.

Driscoll, Mark. *Confessions of a Reformission Rev: Hard Lessons from an Emerging Missional Church*. Grand Rapids: Zondervan, 2006.

Drury, Keith. *The Wonder of Worship: Why We Worship the Way We Do*. Marion, IN: Wesleyan, 2002.

Dulles, Avery. *Models of the Church*. New York: Doubleday, 1987.

Effler, William B. *Turning the Church Inside Out*. N.p.: Worldwide, 2000.

Ford, Marcia. *Traditions of the Ancients: Vintage Faith Practices for the 21st Century*. Nashville: Broadman & Holman, 2006.

Fretheim, Terence E. *God and World in the Old Testament: A Relational Theology of Creation*. Nashville: Abingdon, 2005.

Foster, Richard J. *Celebration of Discipline: The Path to Spiritual Growth*. San Francisco: Harper, 1998.

———. *Prayer: Finding the Heart's True Home*. New York: Harper San Francisco, 1992.

Frost, Michael. *The Road to Missional: Journey to the Center of the Church*. Grand Rapids: Baker, 2011.

Frost, Michael, and Alan Hirsch. *ReJesus: A Wild Messiah for a Missional Church*. Peabody: Hendrickson, 2009.

Gordon, Wayne. *Who is My Neighbor? Lessons Learned from a Man Left for Dead*. Ventura, CA: Gospel Light, 2010.

Green, Chris E. W., ed. *Pentecostal Ecclesiology: A Reader*. Leiden, Netherlands: Brill, 2016.

Greenway, Roger S. "Confronting Urban Contexts with the Gospel." In *Discipling the City: A Comprehensive Approach to Urban Missions*, 35–48. Grand Rapids: Baker, 1992.

Groeschel, Craig. *Divine Direction: 7 Decisions That Will Change Your Life*. Grand Rapids: Zondervan, 2017.

Grunlan, Stephen A., and Marvin Keene Mayers. *Cultural Anthropology: A Christian Perspective*. Grand Rapids: Zondervan, 1988.

Guder, Darrell L. *The Incarnation and the Church's Witness*. Pennsylvania: Trinity, 1999.

———. "Missional Church: From Sending to Being Sent." In *Missional Church: A Vision for the Sending of the Church in North America*, edited by Craig Van Gelder, 1–17. Grand Rapids: Eerdmans, 1998.

Gunton, Colin E. *The Promise of Trinitarian Theology*. Edinburgh, UK: T. & T. Clark, 1991.

Hall, Douglas J. *Thinking the Faith: Christianity Theology in a North American Context*. Minneapolis: Fortress, 1991.

Hawkins, Greg L., and Cally Parkinson. *Focus*. Chicago: Willow Creek, 2009.

Hiebert, Paul G. *Anthropological Insights for Missionaries*. Grand Rapids: Baker, 1985.

———. "Gospel and Culture: The WCC Project." *Missiology: An International Review* 25.2 (1997) 199–207.

———. *The Gospel in Human Contexts: Anthropological Explorations for Contemporary Missions*. Grand Rapids: Baker, 2009.

Houston, Walter J. *Contending for Justice: Ideologies and Theologies of Social Justice in the Old Testament*. New York: T. & T. Clark, 2006.

Hubbard, Robert L., Jr. *The Book of Ruth*. Grand Rapids: Eerdmans, 1988.

Hull, Bill. *The Complete Book of Discipleship*. Colorado Springs: NavPress, 2006.

———. *The Disciple-Making Pastor*. Grand Rapids: Baker, 2007.

Hunter, George G. *How To Reach Secular People*. Nashville: Abingdon, 1992.

Hybels, Bill. *Courageous Leadership*. Grand Rapids: Zondervan, 2002.

Isaacs, Jeremy and Jason Isaacs. *Toxic Soul: A Pastor's Guide to Leading Without Losing Heart*. Canton, GA: Self-published, 2017.

Johnson, Todd M. "Christianity 2017: Five Hundred Years of Protestant Christianity." *International Bulletin of Mission Research* 41.1 (2017) 41–52.

Jones, Lloyd, and D. Martin. *Preaching and Preachers*. Grand Rapids: Zondervan, 2011.

Kimball, Dan. *They Like Jesus but Not the Church: Insights from Emerging Generations*. Grand Rapids: Zondervan, 2007.

Kinnaman, David. *You Lost Me: Why Young Christians Are Leaving Church . . . and Rethinking Faith*. Grand Rapids: Baker, 2011.

Kosmin, Barry. "New Survey Shows College Students are Worried about Economic Prospects: Socially Liberal Millennial Generation sees Perilous Times Ahead." http://commons.trincoll.edu/aris/files/2013/11/ARIS-Student-Survey-Press-Release-2013.pdf.

Kouzes, James M., and Barry Z. Posner. *The Truth about Leadership*. San Francisco: Wiley, 2010.

Kraft, Charles. *Anthropology for Christian Witness*. Maryknoll, NY: Orbis, 1996.

———. *Christianity in Culture: A Study in Dynamic Biblical Theologizing in Cross-Cultural Perspective*. Maryknoll: Orbis, 1986.

LaHaye, Beverly. *Prayer: God's Comfort for Today's Family*. Nashville: Thomas Nelson, 1990.

LeQuire, Stan L, ed. *The Best Preaching on Earth: Sermons on Caring for Creation*. Valley Forge, PA: Judson, 1996.

Limberg, James. *Hosea—Micah*. Atlanta: John Knox, 1988.

Lingenfelter, Sherwood, and Marvin K. Mayers. *Ministering Cross-Culturally: An Incarnational Model for Personal Relationships*. Grand Rapids: Baker, 2003.

Lints, Richard. *Renewing the Evangelical Mission*. Grand Rapids: Erdmans, 2013.

Lockyer, Herbert. *All the Prayers of the Bible*. Grand Rapids: Zondervan, 1959.

Lomenick, Brad. *H3 Leadership: Be Humble. Stay Hungry. Always Hustle*. Nashville: Thomas Nelson, 2015.

London, H. B., Jr., and Neil B. Wiseman. *The Heart of a Great Pastor*. Ventura, CA: Regal, 1994.

Long, Lisa Milligan. "An Exploratory Study of Christian Education and the Personal Apprehension of Eucharist Effect in the Wesleyan Pentecostal Tradition." PhD diss., Biola University, 2017.

Lovejoy, Shawn. *Be Mean About the Vision: Preserving and Protecting What Matters*. Nashville: Thomas Nelson, 2016.

———. *The Measure of Our Success: An Impassioned Plea to Pastors*. Grand Rapids: Baker, 2012.

Lowe, Ben. *Doing Good Without Giving Up: Sustaining Social Action in a World that's Hard to Change.* Downers Grove: InterVarsity, 2014.

―――. *Green Revolution: Coming Together to Care for Creation.* Downers Grove: InterVarsity, 2009.

Luzbetak, Louis J. *The Church and Culture: An Applied Anthropology for the Religious Worker.* Techny, IL: Divine Word, 1970.

Magesa, Laurent. *Anatomy of Inculturation: Transforming the Church in Africa.* Maryknoll, NY: Orbis, 2004.

Marshall, Molly Truman. *Joining the Dance: A Theology of the Spirit.* King of Prussia, PA: Judson, 2003.

Martens, Elmer A. *God's Design: A Focus on Old Testament Theology.* 4th ed. Eugene, OR: Wipf & Stock, 2015.

Mattson, Ingrid. *The Story of the Quran: Its History and Place in Muslim Life.* Malden, MA: Blackwell, 2008.

Maxwell, John C. *The 21 Most Powerful Minutes in a Leader's Day.* Nashville: Thomas Nelson, 2000.

―――. *Partners in Prayer.* Nashville: Thomas Nelson, 1996.

Maynard-Reid, Pedrito U. *Diverse Worship: African American, Caribbean & Hispanic Perspectives.* Downers Grove: InterVarsity, 2000.

McGrath, Alister. "Loving God with the Heart and Mind." http://www.cslewisinstitute. org/Loving_God_Heart_Mind_McGrath.

McKnight, Scott. *A Light Among the Gentiles: Jewish Missionary Activity in the Second Temple Period.* Minneapolis: Fortress, 1991.

Meeks, Douglas. *God the Economist: The Doctrine of God and Political Economy.* Minneapolis: Fortress, 1989.

Merrill, Eugene H. *Deuteronomy.* Nashville: Broodman & Holman, 1994.

Metaxas, Eric. *Bonhoeffer: Pastor, Martyr, Prophet, Spy.* Nashville: Thomas Nelson, 2010.

Migliore, Daniel L. "The Missionary God and the Missionary Church." *Princeton Bulletin* (1998) 14–25.

Moltmann, Jürgen. *The Church in the Power of the Spirit.* Minneapolis: Fortress, 1993.

Moodley, Edley. *Shembe Ancestors and Christ: A Christological Inquiry with Missiological Implications.* Eugene, OR: Pickwick, 2008.

Moore, T. M. *Disciplines of Grace: From Spiritual Routines to Spiritual Renewal.* Downers Grove: InterVarsity Press, 2001.

Moltmann, Jürgen. *God in Creation: A New Theology of Creation and the Spirit of God.* San Francisco: Harper & Row, 1985.

―――. "The Participation of the Church in the History of God." In *The Church in the Power of the Spirit*, translated by Margaret Kohl, 64–65. Minneapolis: Fortress, 1993.

―――. *The Trinity and the Kingdom: The Doctrine of God.* Translated by Margaret Kohl. San Francisco: Harper & Row, 1981.

Nee, Watchman. *What Shall This Man Do?* Fort Washington, PA: Christian Literature Crusade, 1971.

Newbigin, Lesslie. *The Household of God: Lectures on the Nature of the Church.* London: SCM, 1955.

―――. *The Open Secret: An Introduction to the Theology of Missions.* Grand Rapids: Eerdmans, 1995.

―――. *Trinitarian Doctrine for Today's Mission.* Carlisle: Paternoster, 1998.

Niebuhr, Richard H. *Christ and Culture.* New York: Harper, 2001.

———. *Trinitarian Doctrine for Today's Mission*. Carlisle, PA: Paternoster, 1998.

Ogden, Greg. *Unfinished Business: Returning the Ministry to the People of God*. Grand Rapids: Zondervan, 2003.

Packer, James I. "The Calling." In *Baker's Dictionary of Theology*, edited by Everett F Harrison, 108–10. Grand Rapids: Baker, 1960.

Peterson, Eugene, et al. "The Joyful Environmentalists." *Christianity Today*, June 2011.

Pinnock, Clark. *Flame of Love: A Theology of the Holy Spirit*. Downers Grove: InterVarsity, 1996.

Piper, John. *Don't Waste Your Life*. Wheaton, IL: Crossway, 2007.

Platt, David. *Counter Culture: Following Christ in an Anti-Christian Age*. Carol Stream, Illinois: Tyndale, 2017.

Powell, Mark Allan. *Introducing the New Testament: A Historical, Literary, and Theological Survey*. Grand Rapids: Baker, 2009.

Rainer, Thom S. "15 Reasons Our Churches Are Less Evangelistic Today." Lifeway, February 6, 2017. https://www.lifeway.com/pastors/2017/02/06/reasons-churches-less-evangelistic-today/.

Rainer, Thom S., and Eric Geiger. *Simple Church*. Nashville: Broadman & Holman, 2006.

Richards, Randolph E., and Brandon J. O'Brien. *Misreading Scripture with Western Eyes: Removing Cultural Blinders to Better Understand the Bible*. Downers Grove: InterVarsity, 2012.

Richter, Sandra L. "Environmental Law in Deuteronomy: One Lens on a Biblical Theology of Creation Care." *Bulletin for Biblical Research* 203 (2010) 355–76.

Sanneh, Lamin. *Disciples of All Nations: Pillars of World Christianity*. Oxford: Oxford University Press, 2008.

———. *Translating the Message: The Missionary Impact on Culture*. Maryknoll: Orbis, 1996.

Schreiter, Robert. *Constructing Local Theologies*. Maryknoll, NY: Orbis, 1994.

Scroggins, Clay. *How to Lead When You're Not in Charge*. Grand Rapids: Zondervan, 2017.

Senior, Donald, and Carroll Stuhlmueller. *The Biblical Foundations for Mission*. Maryknoll, NY: Orbis, 1995.

Shorter, Allyword. *Toward a Theology of Inculturation: Transforming the Church in Africa*. Maryknoll, NY: Orbis, 1994.

Sider, Ronald J. "Biblical Foundations for Creation Care." In *The Case of Creation*, edited by R. J. Berry, 46. Downers Grove: InterVarsity, 2000.

———. "What if We Defined the Gospel the Way Jesus Did?" In *Holistic Mission: God's Plan for God's People*, edited by Brian Woolnough et al., Eugene, OR: Wipf & Stock, 2010.

Sims, John. *Our Pentecostal Heritage: Reclaiming the Priority of the Holy Spirit*. Cleveland: Pathway, 1995.

Sleeth, J. Matthew. *The Gospel According to the Earth: Why the Good Book Is a Green Book*. New York: HarperOne, 2010.

Small, P. Douglas. *Prayer: The Heart of It All: Biblical Principles with Practical Models*. Kannapolis, NC: Alive, 2017.

Smith, Christian, and Melina Lundquist Denton. *Soul Searching: The Religious and Spiritual Lives of American Teenagers*. Reprint edition. Oxford: Oxford University Press, 2009.

Smith, Sean. *Prophetic Evangelism: Empowering a Generation to Seize Their Day*. Shippensburg, PA: Destiny, 2011.

Snyder, Howard A. *Liberating the Church: The Ecology of Church and Kingdom*. Downers Grove: InterVarsity, 1983.

Steele, Les. *On the Way: A Practical Theology of Christian Formation*. Eugene, OR: Wipf & Stock, 2001.

Stott, John R. W. "The Living God is a Missionary God." In *Perspectives on the World Christian Movement: A Reader*, edited by Ralph D. Winter and Steven C. Hawthorne, 3–9. Hattiesburg, MS: William Carey Library Publishers, 1999.

Thomas, Norman. *Classic Texts in Mission & World Christianity*. Maryknoll, NY: Orbis, 1995.

Toly, Noah J., and Daniel I. Block, eds. *Keeping God's Earth: The Global Environment in Biblical Perspective*. Downers Grove: InterVarsity, 2010.

Torrance, Thomas. *Theology in Reconstruction*. Grand Rapids: Eerdmans, 1965.

Towns, Elmer L., and Vernon M. Whaley. *Worship through the Ages: How the Great Awakenings Shape Evangelical Worship*. Nashville: B & H, 2012.

Van Gelder, Craig. *The Essence of the Church: A Community Created by the Spirit*. Grand Rapids: Baker, 2000.

———. *The Ministry of the Missional Church: A Community Led by the Spirit*. Grand Rapids: Baker, 2007.

Van Gelder, Craig, and Dwight I. Zscheile. *The Missional Church in Perspective: Mapping Trends and Shaping Conversation*. Grand Rapids: Baker, 2011.

Volf, Miroslav. "Human Flourishing." In *Renewing the Evangelical Mission*, edited by Richard Lints, 14–17. Grand Rapids: Eerdmans, 2013.

———. *A Public Faith: How Followers of Christ Should Serve the Common Good*. Grand Rapids: Brazos, 2011.

Walling, Terry. "Power of a Focused Life." In *Prevailing Church Regional Workshop Manual*, 1–12. Alta Loma, CA: Church Resource, 2000.

Weaver, John. "Co-Redeemers: A Theological Basis for Creation Care." In *Perspectives in Religious Studies* 36.2 (Summer 2009) 199–216.

Wegner, Rob, and Jack Magruder. *Missional Moves: 15 Tectonic Shifts that Transform Churches, Communities, and the World*. Grand Rapids: Zondervan, 2012.

Whiteman, Darrell L. "Anthropological Reflections on Contextualizing Theology in a Globalizing World." In *Globalizing Theology: Belief and Practice in an Era of World Christianity*, edited by Craig Ott et al., Grand Rapids: Baker, 2006.

Wilkins, Michael. *In His Image: Reflecting Christ in Everyday Life*. Colorado Springs: NavPress, 1997.

Willard, Dallas. *Renovation of the Heart: Putting on the Character of Christ*. Colorado Springs: NavPress, 2002.

Willimon, William H. *Acts: Interpretation: A Bible Commentary for Teaching and Preaching*. Louisville: John Knox, 1988.

Woolnough, Brian, and Wonsuk Ma. *Holistic Mission: God's Plan for God's People*. Eugene, OR: Wipf & Stock, 2010.

Wright, N. T. *Simply Christian: Why Christianity Makes Sense*. New York: HarperCollins, 2006.

Young, Sarah. *Jesus Calling*. Nashville: Thomas Nelson, 2004.

Zodhiates, Spires, ed. *Hebrew Greek Key Word Study Bible*. NIV edition. Chattanooga, AMG International, 1996.